D0765536

Poetry

Man and Camel, 2006
Blizzard of One, 1998
Dark Harbor, 1993
Reasons for Moving, Darker, & The Sargentville Notebook, 1992
The Continuous Life, 1990
Selected Poems, 1980
The Late Hour, 1978
The Story of Our Lives, 1973
Darker, 1970
Reasons for Moving, 1968
Sleeping with One Eye Open, 1964

Prose

The Weather of Words, 2000
Mr. and Mrs. Baby, 1985
The Monument, 1978

Translations

Looking for Poetry, 2002
Travelling in the Family (with Thomas Colchie), 1986
(Poems by Carlos Drummond de Andrade)
The Owl's Insomnia, 1973 (Poems by Rafael Alberti)

Art Books

Hopper, 2001
William Bailey, 1987
Art of the Real, 1983

For Children

Rembrandt Takes a Walk, 1986
The Night Book, 1985
The Planet of Lost Things, 1982

Anthologies

The Golden Ecco Anthology, 1994
The Best American Poetry 1991 (with David Lehman)
Another Republic, 1976 (with Charles Simic)
New Poetry of Mexico, 1970 (with Octavio Paz)
The Contemporary American Poets, 1969

NEW SELECTED POEMS

New Selected Poems

MARK STRAND

ALFRED A. KNOPF   NEW YORK   2007

THIS IS A BORZOI BOOK
PUBLISHED BY ALFRED A. KNOPF

www.aaknopf.com

Poems included in this collection were originally published
in the following works:
Blizzard of One, copyright © 1998 by Mark Strand (Alfred A. Knopf) • *Continuous
Life*, copyright © 1990 by Mark Strand (Alfred A. Knopf) • *Dark Harbor*,
copyright © 1993 by Mark Strand (Alfred A. Knopf) • *Darker*, copyright © 1968,
1969, 1970 by Mark Strand (Atheneum) • *The Late Hour*, copyright © 1973, 1975,
1976, 1977, 1978 by Mark Strand (Atheneum) • *Man and Camel*, copyright © 2006
by Mark Strand (Alfred A. Knopf) • *Reasons for Moving*, copyright © 1963, 1964,
1965, 1966, 1967, 1968 by Mark Strand (Atheneum) • *Selected Poems*, copyright ©
1979, 1980 by Mark Strand (Atheneum) • *Sleeping with One Eye Open*, copyright ©
1964 by Mark Strand (Stone Wall Press) • *The Story of Our Lives*, copyright © 1971,
1972, 1973 by Mark Strand (Atheneum)

Library of Congress Cataloging-in-Publication Data
Strand, Mark, [date]
[Poems, Selections]
New selected poems / by Mark Strand.—1st ed.
p. cm.
ISBN-13: 978-0-307-26297-4
I. Title.
PS3569.T69A6 2007
811'.54—dc22   2007020741

Manufactured in the United States of America
First Edition

CONTENTS

Acknowledgments   xi

FROM *Sleeping with One Eye Open*

Sleeping with One Eye Open   3
When the Vacation Is Over for Good   5
Violent Storm   6
Old People on the Nursing Home Porch   8
Keeping Things Whole   10
The Whole Story   11
The Tunnel   13

FROM *Reasons for Moving*

The Mailman   17
The Accident   18
The Man in the Tree   21
The Man in the Mirror   23
The Ghost Ship   28
Moontan   30
What to Think Of   32
The Marriage   34
Eating Poetry   36
The Dirty Hand   37

FROM *Darker*

The New Poetry Handbook   43
The Remains   45
Giving Myself Up   46

The Room	47
Letter	48
Nostalgia	49
Tomorrow	50
The Dress	51
The Good Life	52
Black Maps	53
Coming to This	55
The Sleep	56
Breath	57
The Prediction	58
From a Litany	59
My Life	61
My Life by Somebody Else	63
Courtship	64
Not Dying	65
The Way It Is	66

FROM *The Story of Our Lives*

Elegy for My Father	71
In Celebration	78
The Story of Our Lives	79
The Untelling	86

The Monument
97

FROM *The Late Hour*

The Coming of Light	137
Another Place	138
Lines for Winter	139
My Son	140

For Jessica, My Daughter   142
From The Long Sad Party   144
The Late Hour   145
The Story   146
For Her   147
So You Say   148
Poor North   149
Pot Roast   150
The House in French Village   152
The Garden   155
Snowfall   156

FROM *Selected Poems*

Shooting Whales   159
Nights in Hackett's Cove   162
A Morning   163
My Mother on an Evening in Late Summer   164

FROM *The Continuous Life*

The Idea   169
Velocity Meadows   170
A.M.   171
Orpheus Alone   172
Fiction   174
Luminism   175
Life in the Valley   176
The Continuous Life   177
Always   178
Se la vita è sventura . . . ?   179
One Winter Night   181
The History of Poetry   182

The Continental College of Beauty   183
The Midnight Club   184
The Famous Scene   185
Itself Now   186
Reading in Place   187
The End   188

FROM *Dark Harbor*   189

I, VII, VIII, XIV, XVI, XX, XXII, XXIII,
XXVII, XXVIII, XXIX, XXXI, XXXV,
XXXVI, XXXIX, XL, XLIII, XLIV, XLV

FROM *Blizzard of One*

The Beach Hotel   213
Old Man Leaves Party   214
I Will Love the Twenty-first Century   215
The Next Time   216
The Night, the Porch   219
Our Masterpiece Is the Private Life   220
Morning, Noon, and Night   222
A Piece of the Storm   224
A Suite of Appearances   225
Here   229
Two de Chiricos   230
Some Last Words   232
In Memory of Joseph Brodsky   234
What It Was   235
The Delirium Waltz   237
The View   243

FROM *Man and Camel*

The King	247
I Had Been a Polar Explorer	248
Man and Camel	249
Fire	250
The Rose	251
Storm	252
Afterwords	253
Elevator	255
Black Sea	256
Mother and Son	257
Mirror	258
Moon	260
Marsyas	261
My Name	263
Poem After the Seven Last Words	264

ACKNOWLEDGMENTS

*I would like to thank the following people who
during the course of my writing life have
given me encouragement and invaluable advice:
Howard Moss, Donald Justice, Harry and Kathleen
Ford, Jeannette Haien, Richard Howard,
Julia Strand, Rosanna Warren, Jorie Graham,
Lee Rust Brown, Deborah Garrison,
and Tricia Dailey.*

From *Sleeping with One Eye Open*

Sleeping with One Eye Open

Unmoved by what the wind does,
The windows
Are not rattled, nor do the various
Areas
Of the house make their usual racket —
Creak at
The joints, trusses, and studs.
Instead,
They are still. And the maples,
Able
At times to raise havoc,
Evoke
Not a sound from their branches
Clutches.
It's my night to be rattled,
Saddled
With spooks. Even the half-moon
(Half man,
Half dark), on the horizon,
Lies on
Its side casting a fishy light
Which alights
On my floor, lavishly lording
Its morbid
Look over me. Oh, I feel dead,
Folded
Away in my blankets for good, and
Forgotten.

My room is clammy and cold,
Moonhandled
And weird. The shivers
Wash over
Me, shaking my bones, my loose ends
Loosen,
And I lie sleeping with one eye open,
Hoping
That nothing, nothing will happen.

When the Vacation Is Over for Good

It will be strange
Knowing at last it couldn't go on forever,
The certain voice telling us over and over
That nothing would change,

And remembering too,
Because by then it will all be done with, the way
Things were, and how we had wasted time as though
There was nothing to do,

When, in a flash
The weather turned, and the lofty air became
Unbearably heavy, the wind strikingly dumb
And our cities like ash,

And knowing also,
What we never suspected, that it was something like summer
At its most august except that the nights were warmer
And the clouds seemed to glow,

And even then,
Because we will not have changed much, wondering what
Will become of things, and who will be left to do it
All over again,

And somehow trying,
But still unable, to know just what it was
That went so completely wrong, or why it is
We are dying.

Violent Storm

Those who have chosen to pass the night
Entertaining friends
And intimate ideas in the bright,
Commodious rooms of dreams
Will not feel the slightest tremor
Or be wakened by what seems
Only a quirk in the dry run
Of conventional weather. For them,
The long night sweeping over these trees
And houses will have been no more than one
In a series whose end
Only the nervous or morbid consider.
But for us, the wide-awake, who tend
To believe the worst is always waiting
Around the next corner or hiding in the dry,
Unsteady branch of a sick tree, debating
Whether or not to fell the passerby,
It has a sinister air.
How we wish we were sunning ourselves
In a world of familiar views
And fixed conditions, confined
By what we know, and able to refuse
Entry to the unaccounted for. For now,
Deeper and darker than ever, the night unveils
Its dubious plans, and the rain
Beats down in gales
Against the roof. We sit behind
Closed windows, bolted doors,

Unsure and ill at ease
While the loose, untidy wind,
Making an almost human sound, pours
Through the open chambers of the trees.
We cannot take ourselves or what belongs
To us for granted. No longer the exclusive,
Last resorts in which we could unwind,
Lounging in easy chairs,
Recalling the various wrongs
We had been done or spared, our rooms
Seem suddenly mixed up in our affairs.
We do not feel protected
By the walls, nor can we hide
Before the duplicating presence
Of their mirrors, pretending we are the ones who stare
From the other side, collected
In the glassy air.
A cold we never knew invades our bones.
We shake as though the storm were going to hurl us down
Against the flat stones
Of our lives. All other nights
Seem pale compared to this, and the brilliant rise
Of morning after morning seems unthinkable.
Already now the lights
That shared our wakefulness are dimming
And the dark brushes against our eyes.

Old People on the Nursing Home Porch

Able at last to stop
And recall the days it took
To get them here, they sit
On the porch in rockers
Letting the faded light
Of afternoon carry them off.

I see them moving back
And forth over the dullness
Of the past, covering ground
They did not know was there,
And ending up with nothing
Save what might have been.

And so they sit, gazing
Out between the trees
Until in all that vacant
Wash of sky, the wasted
Vision of each one
Comes down to earth again.

It is too late to travel
Or even find a reason
To make it seem worthwhile.
Already now, the evening
Reaches out to take
The aging world away.

And soon the dark will come,
And these tired elders feel
The need to go indoors
Where each will lie alone
In the deep and sheepless
Pastures of a long sleep.

Keeping Things Whole

In a field
I am the absence
of field.
This is
always the case.
Wherever I am
I am what is missing.

When I walk
I part the air
and always
the air moves in
to fill the spaces
where my body's been.

We all have reasons
for moving.
I move
to keep things whole.

The Whole Story

—I'd rather you didn't feel it necessary to tell him, "That's a fire. And what's more, we can't do anything about it, because we're on this train, see?"

How it should happen this way
I am not sure, but you
Are sitting next to me,
Minding your own business
When all of a sudden I see
A fire out the window.

I nudge you and say,
"That's a fire. And what's more,
We can't do anything about it,
Because we're on this train, see?"
You give me an odd look
As though I had said too much.

But for all you know I may
Have a passion for fires,
And travel by train to keep
From having to put them out.
It may be that trains
Can kindle a love of fire.

I might even suspect
That you are a fireman
In disguise. And then again
I might be wrong. Maybe
You are the one
Who loves a good fire. Who knows?

Perhaps you are elsewhere,
Deciding that with no place
To go you should not
Take a train. And I,
Seeing my own face in the window,
May have lied about the fire.

The Tunnel

A man has been standing
in front of my house
for days. I peek at him
from the living room
window and at night,
unable to sleep,
I shine my flashlight
down on the lawn.
He is always there.

After a while
I open the front door
just a crack and order
him out of my yard.
He narrows his eyes
and moans. I slam
the door and dash back
to the kitchen, then up
to the bedroom, then down.

I weep like a schoolgirl
and make obscene gestures
through the window. I
write large suicide notes
and place them so he
can read them easily.
I destroy the living
room furniture to prove
I own nothing of value.

When he seems unmoved
I decide to dig a tunnel
to a neighboring yard.
I seal the basement off
from the upstairs with
a brick wall. I dig hard
and in no time the tunnel
is done. Leaving my pick
and shovel below,

I come out in front of a house
and stand there too tired to
move or even speak, hoping
someone will help me.
I feel I'm being watched
and sometimes I hear
a man's voice,
but nothing is done
and I have been waiting for days.

From *Reasons for Moving*

The Mailman

It is midnight.
He comes up the walk
and knocks at the door.
I rush to greet him.
He stands there weeping,
shaking a letter at me.
He tells me it contains
terrible personal news.
He falls to his knees.
"Forgive me! Forgive me!" he pleads.

I ask him inside.
He wipes his eyes.
His dark blue suit
is like an inkstain
on my crimson couch.
Helpless, nervous, small,
he curls up like a ball
and sleeps while I compose
more letters to myself
in the same vein:

"You shall live
by inflicting pain.
You shall forgive."

The Accident

A train runs over me.
I feel sorry
for the engineer
who crouches down
and whispers in my ear
that he is innocent.

He wipes my forehead,
blows the ashes
from my lips.
My blood steams
in the evening air,
clouding his glasses.

He whispers in my ear
the details of his life—
he has a wife
and child he loves,
he's always been
an engineer.

He talks
until the beam
from someone's flashlight
turns us white.
He stands.
He shakes his jacket out

and starts to run.
The cinders crack
under his boots,
the air is cold
and thick
against his cheeks.

Back home he sits
in the kitchen,
staring at the dark.
His face is flushed,
his hands are pressed
between his knees.

He sees me sprawled
and motionless
beside the tracks
and the faint blooms
of my breath
being swept away;

the fields bend
under the heavy sheets
of the wind
and birds scatter
into the rafters
of the trees.

He rushes
from the house,
lifts the wreckage
of my body in his arms,

and brings me back.
I lie in bed.

He puts his head
down next to mine
and tells me
that I'll be all right.
A pale light
shines in his eyes.

I listen to the wind
press hard against the house.
I cannot sleep.
I cannot stay awake.
The shutters bang.
The end of my life begins.

The Man in the Tree

I sat in the cold limbs of a tree.
I wore no clothes and the wind was blowing.
You stood below in a heavy coat,
the coat you are wearing.

And when you opened it, baring your chest,
white moths flew out, and whatever you said
at that moment fell quietly onto the ground,
the ground at your feet.

Snow floated down from the clouds into my ears.
The moths from your coat flew into the snow.
And the wind as it moved under my arms, under my chin,
whined like a child.

I shall never know why
our lives took a turn for the worse, nor will you.
Clouds sank into my arms and my arms rose.
They are rising now.

I sway in the white air of winter
and the starling's cry lies down on my skin.
A field of ferns covers my glasses; I wipe them away
in order to see you.

I turn and the tree turns with me.
Things are not only themselves in this light.
You close your eyes and your coat
falls from your shoulders,

the tree withdraws like a hand,
the wind fits into my breath, yet nothing is certain.
The poem that has stolen these words from my mouth
may not be this poem.

The Man in the Mirror

for Decio de Souza

I walk down the narrow,
carpeted hall.
The house is set.
The carnation in my buttonhole

precedes me like a small
continuous explosion.
The mirror
is in the living room.

You are there.
Your face is white, unsmiling, swollen.
The fallen body of your hair
is dull and out of place.

Buried in the darkness of your pockets,
your hands are motionless.
You do not seem awake.
Your skin sleeps

and your eyes lie in the deep
blue of their sockets,
impossible to reach.
How long will all this take?

I remember how we used to stand
wishing the glass
would dissolve between us,
and how we watched our words

cloud that bland,
innocent surface,
and when our faces blurred
how scared we were.

But that was another life.
One day you turned away
and left me here
to founder in the stillness of your wake.

Your suit floating, your hair
moving like eel grass
in a shallow bay, you drifted
out of the mirror's room, through the hall,

and into the open air.
You seemed to rise and fall
with the wind, the sway
taking you always farther away, farther away.

Darkness filled your sleeves.
The stars moved through you.
The vague music of your shrieking
blossomed in my ears.

I tried forgetting what I saw;
I got down on the floor,
pretending to be dead.
It did not work.

My heart bunched in my rib-cage like a bat,
blind and cowardly,
beating in and out,
a solemn, irreducible black.

The things you drove me to!
I walked in the calm of the house,
calling you back.
You did not answer.

I sat in a chair
and stared across the room.
The walls were bare.
The mirror was nothing without you.

I lay down on the couch
and closed my eyes.
My thoughts rose in the dark
like faint balloons,

and I would turn them over
one by one and watch them shiver.
I always fell into a deep
and arid sleep.

Then out of nowhere late one night
you reappeared,
a huge vegetable moon,
a bruise coated with light.

You stood before me,
dreamlike and obscene,
your face lost
under layers of heavy skin,

your body sunk in a green
and wrinkled sea of clothing.
I tried to help you
but you refused.

Days passed
and I would rest
my cheek against the glass,
wanting nothing but the old you.

I sang so sadly
that the neighbors wept
and dogs whined with pity.
Some things I wish I could forget.

You didn't care,
standing still while flies
collected in your hair
and dust fell like a screen before your eyes.

You never spoke
or tried to come up close.
Why did I want so badly
to get through to you?

It still goes on.
I go into the living room and you are there.
You drift in a pool
of silver air

where wounds and dreams of wounds
rise from the deep
humus of sleep
to bloom like flowers against the glass.

I look at you
and see myself
under the surface.
A dark and private weather

settles down on everything.
It is colder
and the dreams wither away.
You stand

like a shade
in the painless glass,
frail, distant, older
than ever.

It will always be this way.
I stand here scared
that you will disappear,
scared that you will stay.

The Ghost Ship

Through the crowded street
It floats,

Its vague
Tonnage like wind.

It glides
Through the sadness

Of slums
To the outlying fields.

Slowly,
Now by an ox,

Now by a windmill,
It moves.

Passing
At night like a dream

Of death,
It cannot be heard;

Under the stars
It steals.

Its crew
And passengers stare;

Whiter than bone,
Their eyes

Do not
Turn or close.

Moontan

for Donald Justice

The bluish, pale
face of the house
rises above me
like a wall of ice

and the distant,
solitary
barking of an owl
floats toward me.

I half close my eyes.

Over the damp
dark of the garden
flowers swing
back and forth
like small balloons.

The solemn trees,
each buried
in a cloud of leaves,
seem lost in sleep.

It is late.
I lie in the grass,
smoking,
feeling at ease,
pretending the end
will be like this.

Moonlight
falls on my flesh.
A breeze
circles my wrist.

I drift.
I shiver.
I know that soon
the day will come
to wash away the moon's
white stain,

that I shall walk
in the morning sun
invisible
as anyone.

What to Think Of

Think of the jungle,
The green steam rising.

It is yours.
You are the prince of Paraguay.

Your minions kneel
Deep in the shade of giant leaves

While you drive by
Benevolent as gold.

They kiss the air
That moments before

Swept over your skin,
And rise only after you've passed.

Think of yourself, almost a god,
Your hair on fire,

The bellows of your heart pumping.
Think of the bats

Rushing out of their caves
Like a dark wind to greet you;

Of the vast nocturnal cities
Of lightning bugs

Floating down
From Minas Gerais;

Of the coral snakes;
Of the crimson birds

With emerald beaks;
Of the tons and tons of morpho butterflies

Filling the air
Like the cold confetti of paradise.

The Marriage

The wind comes from opposite poles,
traveling slowly.

She turns in the deep air.
He walks in the clouds.

She readies herself,
shakes out her hair,

makes up her eyes,
smiles.

The sun warms her teeth,
the tip of her tongue moistens them.

He brushes the dust from his suit
and straightens his tie.

He smokes.
Soon they will meet.

The wind carries them closer.
They wave.

Closer, closer.
They embrace.

She is making a bed.
He is pulling off his pants.

They marry
and have a child.

The wind carries them off
in different directions.

The wind is strong, he thinks
as he straightens his tie.

I like this wind, she says
as she puts on her dress.

The wind unfolds.
The wind is everything to them.

Eating Poetry

Ink runs from the corners of my mouth.
There is no happiness like mine.
I have been eating poetry.

The librarian does not believe what she sees.
Her eyes are sad
and she walks with her hands in her dress.

The poems are gone.
The light is dim.
The dogs are on the basement stairs and coming up.

Their eyeballs roll,
their blond legs burn like brush.
The poor librarian begins to stamp her feet and weep.

She does not understand.
When I get on my knees and lick her hand,
she screams.

I am a new man.
I snarl at her and bark.
I romp with joy in the bookish dark.

The Dirty Hand

(after Carlos Drummond de Andrade)

My hand is dirty.
I must cut it off.
To wash it is pointless.
The water is putrid.
The soap is bad.
It won't lather.
The hand is dirty.
It's been dirty for years.

I used to keep it
out of sight,
in my pants pocket.
No one suspected a thing.
People came up to me,
wanting to shake hands.
I would refuse
and the hidden hand,
like a dark slug,
would leave its imprint
on my thigh.
And then I realized
it was the same
if I used it or not.
Disgust was the same.

How many nights
in the depths of the house
I washed that hand,

scrubbed it, polished it,
dreamed it would turn
to diamond or crystal
or even, at last,
into a plain white hand,
the clean hand of a man,
that you could shake,
or kiss, or hold
in one of those moments
when two people confess
without saying a word . . .
Only to have
the incurable hand,
lethargic and crablike,
open its dirty fingers.

And the dirt was vile.
It was not mud or soot
or the caked filth
of an old scab
or the sweat
of a laborer's shirt.
It was a sad dirt
made of sickness
and human anguish.
It was not black;
black is pure.
It was dull,
a dull grayish dirt.

It is impossible
to live with this
gross hand that lies

on the table.
Quick! Cut it off!
Chop it to pieces
and throw it
into the ocean.
With time, with hope
and its intricate workings,
another hand will come,
pure, transparent as glass,
and fasten itself to my arm.

From *Darker*

The New Poetry Handbook

for Greg Orr and Greg Simon

1 If a man understands a poem,
      he shall have troubles.

2 If a man lives with a poem,
      he shall die lonely.

3 If a man lives with two poems,
      he shall be unfaithful to one.

4 If a man conceives of a poem,
      he shall have one less child.

5 If a man conceives of two poems,
      he shall have two children less.

6 If a man wears a crown on his head as he writes,
      he shall be found out.

7 If a man wears no crown on his head as he writes,
      he shall deceive no one but himself.

8 If a man gets angry at a poem,
      he shall be scorned by men.

9 If a man continues to be angry at a poem,
      he shall be scorned by women.

10 If a man publicly denounces poetry,
      his shoes will fill with urine.

43

11 If a man gives up poetry for power,
        he shall have lots of power.

12 If a man brags about his poems,
        he shall be loved by fools.

13 If a man brags about his poems and loves fools,
        he shall write no more.

14 If a man craves attention because of his poems,
        he shall be like a jackass in moonlight.

15 If a man writes a poem and praises the poem of a fellow,
        he shall have a beautiful mistress.

16 If a man writes a poem and praises the poem of a fellow overly,
        he shall drive his mistress away.

17 If a man claims the poem of another,
        his heart shall double in size.

18 If a man lets his poems go naked,
        he shall fear death.

19 If a man fears death,
        he shall be saved by his poems.

20 If a man does not fear death,
        he may or may not be saved by his poems.

21 If a man finishes a poem,
        he shall bathe in the blank wake of his passion and be kissed
            by white paper.

The Remains

for Bill and Sandy Bailey

I empty myself of the names of others. I empty my pockets.
I empty my shoes and leave them beside the road.
At night I turn back the clocks;
I open the family album and look at myself as a boy.

What good does it do? The hours have done their job.
I say my own name. I say goodbye.
The words follow each other downwind.
I love my wife but send her away.

My parents rise out of their thrones
into the milky rooms of clouds. How can I sing?
Time tells me what I am. I change and I am the same.
I empty myself of my life and my life remains.

Giving Myself Up

I give up my eyes which are glass eggs.
I give up my tongue.
I give up my mouth which is the constant dream of my tongue.
I give up my throat which is the sleeve of my voice.
I give up my heart which is a burning apple.
I give up my lungs which are trees that have never seen the moon.
I give up my smell which is that of a stone traveling through rain.
I give up my hands which are ten wishes.
I give up my arms which have wanted to leave me anyway.
I give up my legs which are lovers only at night.
I give up my buttocks which are the moons of childhood.
I give up my penis which whispers encouragement to my thighs.
I give up my clothes which are walls that blow in the wind
        and I give up the ghost that lives in them.
I give up. I give up.
And you will have none of it because already I am beginning
again without anything.

The Room

It is an old story, the way it happens
sometimes in winter, sometimes not.
The listener falls asleep,
the doors to the closets of his unhappiness open,

and into his room the misfortunes come—
death by daybreak, death by nightfall,
their wooden wings bruising the air,
their shadows the spilled milk the world cries over.

There is a need for surprise endings;
the green field where cows burn like newsprint,
where the farmer sits and stares,
where nothing, when it happens, is never terrible enough.

Letter

for Richard Howard

Men are running across a field,
pens fall from their pockets.
People out walking will pick them up.
It is one of the ways letters are written.

How things fall to others!
The self no longer belonging to me, but asleep
in a stranger's shadow, now clothing
the stranger, now leading him off.

It is noon as I write to you.
Someone's life has come into my hands.
The sun whitens the buildings.
It is all I have. I give it all to you. Yours,

Nostalgia

for Donald Justice

The professors of English have taken their gowns
to the laundry, have taken themselves to the fields.
Dreams of motion circle the Persian rug in a room you were in.
On the beach the sadness of gramophones
deepens the ocean's folding and falling.
It is yesterday. It is still yesterday.

Tomorrow

Your best friend is gone,
your other friend, too.
Now the dream that used to turn in your sleep
sails into the year's coldest night.

What did you say?
Or was it something you did?
It makes no difference—the house of breath collapsing
around your voice, your voice burning, are nothing to worry about.

Tomorrow your friends will come back;
your moist open mouth will bloom in the glass of storefronts.
Yes. Yes. Tomorrow they will come back and you
will invent an ending that comes out right.

The Dress

Lie down on the bright hill
with the moon's hand on your cheek,
your flesh deep in the white folds of your dress,
and you will not hear the passionate mole
extending the length of his darkness,
or the owl arranging all of the night,
which is his wisdom, or the poem
filling your pillow with its blue feathers.
But if you step out of your dress and move into the shade,
the mole will find you, so will the owl, and so will the poem,
and you will fall into another darkness, one you will find
yourself making and remaking until it is perfect.

The Good Life

You stand at the window.
There is a glass cloud in the shape of a heart.
The wind's sighs are like caves in your speech.
You are the ghost in the tree outside.

The street is quiet.
The weather, like tomorrow, like your life,
is partially here, partially up in the air.
There is nothing you can do.

The good life gives no warning.
It weathers the climates of despair
and appears, on foot, unrecognized, offering nothing,
and you are there.

Black Maps

Not the attendance of stones,
nor the applauding wind,
shall let you know
you have arrived,

nor the sea that celebrates
only departures,
nor the mountains,
nor the dying cities.

Nothing will tell you
where you are.
Each moment is a place
you've never been.

You can walk
believing you cast
a light around you.
But how will you know?

The present is always dark.
Its maps are black,
rising from nothing,
describing,

in their slow ascent
into themselves,
their own voyage,
its emptiness,

the bleak, temperate
necessity of its completion.
As they rise into being
they are like breath.

And if they are studied at all
it is only to find,
too late, what you thought
were concerns of yours

do not exist.
Your house is not marked
on any of them,
nor are your friends,

waiting for you to appear,
nor are your enemies,
listing your faults.
Only you are there,

saying hello
to what you will be,
and the black grass
is holding up the black stars.

Coming to This

We have done what we wanted.
We have discarded dreams, preferring the heavy industry
of each other, and we have welcomed grief
and called ruin the impossible habit to break.

And now we are here.
The dinner is ready and we cannot eat.
The meat sits in the white lake of its dish.
The wine waits.

Coming to this
has its rewards: nothing is promised, nothing is taken away.
We have no heart or saving grace,
no place to go, no reason to remain.

The Sleep

There is the sleep of my tongue
speaking a language I can never remember—
words that enter the sleep of words
once they are spoken.

There is the sleep of one moment
inside the next, lengthening the night,
and the sleep of the window
turning the tall sleep of trees into glass.

The sleep of novels as they are read is soundless
like the sleep of dresses on the warm bodies of women.
And the sleep of thunder gathering dust on sunny days
and the sleep of ashes long after.

The sleep of wind has been known to fill the sky.
The long sleep of air locked in the lungs of the dead.
The sleep of a room with someone inside it.
Even the wooden sleep of the moon is possible.

And there is the sleep that demands I lie down
and be fitted to the dark that comes upon me
like another skin in which I shall never be found,
out of which I shall never appear.

Breath

When you see them
tell them I am still here,
that I stand on one leg while the other one dreams,
that this is the only way,

that the lies I tell them are different
from the lies I tell myself,
that by being both here and beyond
I am becoming a horizon,

that as the sun rises and sets I know my place,
that breath is what saves me,
that even the forced syllables of decline are breath,
that if the body is a coffin it is also a closet of breath,

that breath is a mirror clouded by words,
that breath is all that survives the cry for help
as it enters the stranger's ear
and stays long after the word is gone,

that breath is the beginning again, that from it
all resistance falls away, as meaning falls
away from life, or darkness falls from light,
that breath is what I give them when I send my love.

The Prediction

That night the moon drifted over the pond,
turning the water to milk, and under
the boughs of the trees, the blue trees,
a young woman walked, and for an instant

the future came to her:
rain falling on her husband's grave, rain falling
on the lawns of her children, her own mouth
filling with cold air, strangers moving into her house,

a man in her room writing a poem, the moon drifting into it,
a woman strolling under its trees, thinking of death,
thinking of him thinking of her, and the wind rising
and taking the moon and leaving the paper dark.

From a Litany

There in an open field I lie down in a hole I once dug and I praise
 the sky.
I praise the clouds that are like lungs of light.
I praise the owl that wants to inhabit me and the hawk that does not.
I praise the mouse's fury, the wolf's consideration.
I praise the dog that lives in the household of people and shall never
 be one of them.
I praise the whale that lives under the cold blankets of salt.
I praise the formations of squid, the domes of meandra.
I praise the secrecy of doors, the openness of windows.
I praise the depth of closets.
I praise the wind, the rising generations of air.
I praise the trees on whose branches shall sit the Cock of Portugal and
 the Polish Cock.
I praise the palm trees of Rio and those that shall grow in London.
I praise the gardeners, the worms and the small plants that praise
 each other.
I praise the sweet berries of Georgetown, Maine, and the song of the
 white-throated sparrow.
I praise the poets of Waverly Place and Eleventh Street, and the one
 whose bones turn to dark emeralds when he stands upright in the
 wind.
I praise the clocks for which I grow old in a day and young in a day.
I praise all manner of shade, that which I see and that which I do not.
I praise all roofs from the watery roof of the pond to the slate roof of
 the customs house.
I praise those who have made of their bodies final embassies of flesh.

I praise the failure of those with ambition, the authors of leaflets and
     notebooks of nothing.
I praise the moon for suffering men.
I praise the sun its tributes.
I praise the pain of revival and the bliss of decline.
I praise all for nothing because there is no price.
I praise myself for the way I have with a shovel and I praise the shovel.
I praise the motive of praise by which I shall be reborn.
I praise the morning whose sun is upon me.
I praise the evening whose son I am.

My Life

The huge doll of my body
refuses to rise.
I am the toy of women.
My mother

would prop me up for her friends.
"Talk, talk," she would beg.
I moved my mouth
but words did not come.

My wife took me down from the shelf.
I lay in her arms. "We suffer
the sickness of self," she would whisper.
And I lay there dumb.

Now my daughter
gives me a plastic nurser
filled with water.
"You are my real baby," she says.

Poor child!
I look into the brown
mirrors of her eyes
and see myself

diminishing, sinking down
to a depth she does not know is there.
Out of breath,
I will not rise again.

I grow into my death.
My life is small
and getting smaller. The world is green.
Nothing is all.

My Life by Somebody Else

I have done what I could but you avoid me.
I left a bowl of milk on the desk to tempt you.
Nothing happened. I left my wallet there, full of money.
You must have hated me for that. You never came.

I sat at my typewriter naked, hoping you would wrestle me
to the floor. I played with myself just to arouse you.
Boredom drove me to sleep. I offered you my wife.
I sat her on the desk and spread her legs. I waited.

The days drag on. The exhausted light falls like a bandage
over my eyes. Is it because I am ugly? Was anyone
ever so sad? It is pointless to slash my wrists. My hands
would fall off. And then what hope would I have?

Why do you never come? Must I have you by being
somebody else? Must I write *My Life* by somebody else?
My Death by somebody else? Are you listening?
Somebody else has arrived. Somebody else is writing.

Courtship

There is a girl you like so you tell her
your penis is big, but that you cannot get yourself
to use it. Its demands are ridiculous, you say,
even self-defeating, but to be honored somehow,
briefly, inconspicuously, in the dark.

When she closes her eyes in horror,
you take it all back. You tell her you're almost
a girl yourself and can understand why she is shocked.
When she is about to walk away, you tell her
you have no penis, that you don't

know what got into you. You get on your knees.
She suddenly bends down to kiss your shoulder and you know
you're on the right track. You tell her you want
to bear children and that is why you seem confused.
You wrinkle your brow and curse the day you were born.

She tries to calm you, but you lose control.
You reach for her panties and beg forgiveness as you do.
She squirms and you howl like a wolf. Your craving
seems monumental. You know you will have her.
Taken by storm, she is the girl you will marry.

Not Dying

These wrinkles are nothing.
These gray hairs are nothing.
This stomach which sags
with old food, these bruised
and swollen ankles,
my darkening brain,
they are nothing.
I am the same boy
my mother used to kiss.

The years change nothing.
On windless summer nights
I feel those kisses
slide from her dark
lips far away,
and in winter they float
over the frozen pines
and arrive covered with snow.
They keep me young.

My passion for milk
is uncontrollable still.
I am driven by innocence.
From bed to chair I crawl
and back again.
I shall not die.
The grave result
and token of birth, my body
remembers and holds fast.

The Way It Is

The world is ugly,
And the people are sad.

WALLACE STEVENS

I lie in bed.
I toss all night
in the cold unruffled deep
of my sheets and cannot sleep.

My neighbor marches in his room,
wearing the sleek
mask of a hawk with a large beak.
He stands by the window. A violet plume

rises from his helmet's dome.
The moon's light
spills over him like milk and the wind rinses the white
glass bowls of his eyes.

His helmet in a shopping bag,
he sits in the park, waving a small American flag.
He cannot be heard as he moves
behind trees and hedges,

always at the frayed edges
of town, pulling a gun on someone like me. I crouch
under the kitchen table, telling myself
I am a dog, who would kill a dog?

My neighbor's wife comes home.
She walks into the living room,
takes off her clothes, her hair falls down her back.
She seems to wade

through long flat rivers of shade.
The soles of her feet are black.
She kisses her husband's neck
and puts her hands inside his pants.

My neighbors dance.
They roll on the floor, his tongue
is in her ear, his lungs
reek with the swill and weather of hell.

Out on the street people are lying down
with their knees in the air, tears
fill their eyes, ashes
enter their ears.

Their clothes are torn
from their backs. Their faces are worn.
Horsemen are riding around them, telling them why
they should die.

My neighbor's wife calls to me, her mouth is pressed
against the wall behind my bed.
She says, "My husband's dead."
I turn over on my side,

hoping she has not lied.
The walls and ceiling of my room are gray—
the moon's color through the windows of a laundromat.
I close my eyes.

I see myself float
on the dead sea of my bed, falling away,
calling for help, but the vague scream
sticks in my throat.

I see myself in the park
on horseback, surrounded by dark,
leading the armies of peace.
The iron legs of the horse do not bend.

I drop the reins. Where will the turmoil end?
Fleets of taxis stall
in the fog, passengers fall
asleep. Gas pours

from a tricolored stack.
Locking their doors,
people from offices huddle together,
telling the same story over and over.

Everyone who has sold himself wants to buy himself back.
Nothing is done. The night
eats into their limbs
like a blight.

Everything dims.
The future is not what it used to be.
The graves are ready. The dead
shall inherit the dead.

From *The Story of Our Lives*

Elegy for My Father
Robert Strand 1908–1968

I   THE EMPTY BODY

The hands were yours, the arms were yours,
But you were not there.
The eyes were yours, but they were closed and would not open.
The distant sun was there.
The moon poised on the hill's white shoulder was there.
The wind on Bedford Basin was there.
The pale green light of winter was there.
Your mouth was there,
But you were not there.
When somebody spoke, there was no answer.
Clouds came down
And buried the buildings along the water,
And the water was silent.
The gulls stared.
The years, the hours, that would not find you
Turned in the wrists of others.
There was no pain. It had gone.
There were no secrets. There was nothing to say.
The shade scattered its ashes.
The body was yours, but you were not there.
The air shivered against its skin.
The dark leaned into its eyes.
But you were not there.

Why did you travel?
Because the house was cold.
Why did you travel?
Because it is what I have always done between sunset and sunrise.
What did you wear?
I wore a blue suit, a white shirt, yellow tie, and yellow socks.
What did you wear?
I wore nothing. A scarf of pain kept me warm.
Who did you sleep with?
I slept with a different woman each night.
Who did you sleep with?
I slept alone. I have always slept alone.
Why did you lie to me?
I always thought I told the truth.
Why did you lie to me?
Because the truth lies like nothing else and I love the truth.
Why are you going?
Because nothing means much to me anymore.
Why are you going?
I don't know. I have never known.
How long shall I wait for you?
Do not wait for me. I am tired and I want to lie down.
Are you tired and do you want to lie down?
Yes, I am tired and I want to lie down.

3   YOUR DYING

Nothing could stop you.
Not the best day. Not the quiet. Not the ocean rocking.
You went on with your dying.
Not the trees

Under which you walked, not the trees that shaded you.
Not the doctor
Who warned you, the white-haired young doctor who saved you once.
You went on with your dying.
Nothing could stop you. Not your son. Not your daughter
Who fed you and made you into a child again.
Not your son who thought you would live forever.
Not the wind that shook your lapels.
Not the stillness that offered itself to your motion.
Not your shoes that grew heavier.
Not your eyes that refused to look ahead.
Nothing could stop you.
You sat in your room and stared at the city
And went on with your dying.
You went to work and let the cold enter your clothes.
You let blood seep into your socks.
Your face turned white.
Your voice cracked in two.
You leaned on your cane.
But nothing could stop you.
Not your friends who gave you advice.
Not your son. Not your daughter who watched you grow small.
Not fatigue that lived in your sighs.
Not your lungs that would fill with water.
Not your sleeves that carried the pain of your arms.
Nothing could stop you.
You went on with your dying.
When you played with children you went on with your dying.
When you sat down to eat,
When you woke up at night, wet with tears, your body sobbing,
You went on with your dying.
Nothing could stop you.
Not the past.

Not the future with its good weather.
Not the view from your window, the view of the graveyard.
Not the city. Not the terrible city with its wooden buildings.
Not defeat. Not success.
You did nothing but go on with your dying.
You put your watch to your ear.
You felt yourself slipping.
You lay on the bed.
You folded your arms over your chest and you dreamed of the world
  without you,
Of the space under the trees,
Of the space in your room,
Of the spaces that would now be empty of you,
And you went on with your dying.
Nothing could stop you.
Not your breathing. Not your life.
Not the life you wanted.
Not the life you had.
Nothing could stop you.

4   YOUR SHADOW

You have your shadow.
The places where you were have given it back.
The hallways and bare lawns of the orphanage have given it back.
The Newsboys' Home has given it back.
The streets of New York have given it back and so have the streets of
  Montreal.
The rooms in Belém where lizards would snap at mosquitoes have
  given it back.
The dark streets of Manaus and the damp streets of Rio have given
  it back.
Mexico City where you wanted to leave it has given it back.

And Halifax where the harbor would wash its hands of you has given
   it back.
You have your shadow.
When you traveled the white wake of your going sent your shadow
   below, but when you arrived it was there to greet you. You had
   your shadow.
The doorways you entered lifted your shadow from you and when
   you went out, gave it back. You had your shadow.
Even when you forgot your shadow, you found it again; it had been
   with you.
Once in the country the shade of a tree covered your shadow and you
   were not known.
Once in the country you thought your shadow had been cast by
   somebody else. Your shadow said nothing.
Your clothes carried your shadow inside; when you took them off, it
   spread like the dark of your past.
And your words that float like leaves in an air that is lost, in a place no
   one knows, gave you back your shadow.
Your friends gave you back your shadow.
Your enemies gave you back your shadow. They said it was heavy and
   would cover your grave.
When you died your shadow slept at the mouth of the furnace and ate
   ashes for bread.
It rejoiced among ruins.
It watched while others slept.
It shone like crystal among the tombs.
It composed itself like air.
It wanted to be like snow on water.
It wanted to be nothing, but that was not possible.
It came to my house.
It sat on my shoulders.
Your shadow is yours. I told it so. I said it was yours.
I have carried it with me too long. I give it back.

They mourn for you.
When you rise at midnight,
And the dew glitters on the stone of your cheeks,
They mourn for you.
They lead you back into the empty house.
They carry the chairs and tables inside.
They sit you down and teach you to breathe.
And your breath burns,
It burns the pine box and the ashes fall like sunlight.
They give you a book and tell you to read.
They listen and their eyes fill with tears.
The women stroke your fingers.
They comb the yellow back into your hair.
They shave the frost from your beard.
They knead your thighs.
They dress you in fine clothes.
They rub your hands to keep them warm.
They feed you. They offer you money.
They get on their knees and beg you not to die.
When you rise at midnight they mourn for you.
They close their eyes and whisper your name over and over.
But they cannot drag the buried light from your veins.
Old man, rise and keep rising, it does no good.
They mourn for you the way they can.

6   THE NEW YEAR

It is winter and the new year.
Nobody knows you.
Away from the stars, from the rain of light,
You lie under the weather of stones.

There is no thread to lead you back.
Your friends doze in the dark
Of pleasure and cannot remember.
Nobody knows you. You are the neighbor of nothing.
You do not see the rain falling and the man walking away,
The soiled wind blowing its ashes across the city.
You do not see the sun dragging the moon like an echo.
You do not see the bruised heart go up in flames,
The skulls of the innocent turn into smoke.
You do not see the scars of plenty, the eyes without light.
It is over. It is winter and the new year.
The meek are hauling their skins into heaven.
The hopeless are suffering the cold with those who have nothing
    to hide.
It is over and nobody knows you.
There is starlight drifting on the black water.
There are stones in the sea no one has seen.
There is a shore and people are waiting.
And nothing comes back.
Because it is over.
Because there is silence instead of a name.
Because it is winter and the new year.

In Celebration

You sit in a chair, touched by nothing, feeling
the old self become the older self, imagining
only the patience of water, the boredom of stone.
You think that silence is the extra page,
you think that nothing is good or bad, not even
the darkness that fills the house while you sit watching
it happen. You've seen it happen before. Your friends
move past the window, their faces soiled with regret.
You want to wave but cannot raise your hand.
You sit in a chair. You turn to the nightshade spreading
a poisonous net around the house. You taste
the honey of absence. It is the same wherever
you are, the same if the voice rots before
the body, or the body rots before the voice.
You know that desire leads only to sorrow, that sorrow
leads to achievement which leads to emptiness.
You know that this is different, that this
is the celebration, the only celebration,
that by giving yourself over to nothing,
you shall be healed. You know there is joy in feeling
your lungs prepare themselves for an ashen future,
so you wait, you stare and you wait, and the dust settles
and the miraculous hours of childhood wander in darkness.

The Story of Our Lives

for Howard Moss

1

We are reading the story of our lives
which takes place in a room.
The room looks out on a street.
There is no one there,
no sound of anything.
The trees are heavy with leaves,
the parked cars never move.
We keep turning the pages,
hoping for something,
something like mercy or change,
a black line that would bind us
or keep us apart.
The way it is, it would seem
the book of our lives is empty.
The furniture in the room is never shifted,
and the rugs become darker each time
our shadows pass over them.
It is almost as if the room were the world.
We sit beside each other on the couch,
reading about the couch.
We say it is ideal.
It is ideal.

2

We are reading the story of our lives
as though we were in it,

79

as though we had written it.
This comes up again and again.
In one of the chapters
I lean back and push the book aside
because the book says
it is what I am doing.
I lean back and begin to write about the book.
I write that I wish to move beyond the book,
beyond my life into another life.
I put the pen down.
The book says: *He put the pen down*
and turned and watched her reading
the part about herself falling in love.
The book is more accurate than we can imagine.
I lean back and watch you read
about the man across the street.
They built a house there,
and one day a man walked out of it.
You fell in love with him
because you knew that he would never visit you,
would never know you were waiting.
Night after night you would say
that he was like me.
I lean back and watch you grow older without me.
Sunlight falls on your silver hair.
The rugs, the furniture,
seem almost imaginary now.
She continued to read.
She seemed to consider his absence
of no special importance,
as someone on a perfect day will consider
the weather a failure
because it did not change his mind.

You narrow your eyes.
You have the impulse to close the book
which describes my resistance:
how when I lean back I imagine
my life without you, imagine moving
into another life, another book.
It describes your dependence on desire,
how the momentary disclosures
of purpose make you afraid.
The book describes much more than it should.
It wants to divide us.

3

This morning I woke and believed
there was no more to our lives
than the story of our lives.
When you disagreed, I pointed
to the place in the book where you disagreed.
You fell back to sleep and I began to read
those mysterious parts you used to guess at
while they were being written
and lose interest in after they became
part of the story.
In one of them cold dresses of moonlight
are draped over the chairs in a man's room.
He dreams of a woman whose dresses are lost,
who sits in a garden and waits.
She believes that love is a sacrifice.
The part describes her death
and she is never named,
which is one of the things
you could not stand about her.

A little later we learn
that the dreaming man lives
in the new house across the street.
This morning after you fell back to sleep
I began to turn pages early in the book:
it was like dreaming of childhood,
so much seemed to vanish,
so much seemed to come to life again.
I did not know what to do.
The book said: *In those moments it was his book.*
A bleak crown rested uneasily on his head.
He was the brief ruler of inner and outer discord,
anxious in his own kingdom.

4

Before you woke
I read another part that described your absence
and told how you sleep to reverse
the progress of your life.
I was touched by my own loneliness as I read,
knowing that what I feel is often the crude
and unsuccessful form of a story
that may never be told.
I read and was moved by a desire to offer myself
to the house of your sleep.
He wanted to see her naked and vulnerable,
to see her in the refuse, the discarded
plots of old dreams, the costumes and masks
of unattainable states.
It was as if he were drawn
irresistibly to failure.
It was hard to keep reading.

I was tired and wanted to give up.
The book seemed aware of this.
It hinted at changing the subject.
I waited for you to wake not knowing
how long I waited,
and it seemed that I was no longer reading.
I heard the wind passing
like a stream of sighs
and I heard the shiver of leaves
in the trees outside the window.
It would be in the book.
Everything would be there.
I looked at your face
and I read the eyes, the nose, the mouth . . .

5

If only there were a perfect moment in the book;
if only we could live in that moment,
we could begin the book again
as if we had not written it,
as if we were not in it.
But the dark approaches
to any page are too numerous
and the escapes are too narrow.
We read through the day.
Each page turning is like a candle
moving through the mind.
Each moment is like a hopeless cause.
If only we could stop reading.
He never wanted to read another book
and she kept staring into the street.
The cars were still there,

the deep shade of trees covered them.
The shades were drawn in the new house.
Maybe the man who lived there,
the man she loved, was reading
the story of another life.
She imagined a bare parlor,
a cold fireplace, a man sitting
writing a letter to a woman
who has sacrificed her life for love.
If there were a perfect moment in the book,
it would be the last.
The book never discusses the causes of love.
It claims confusion is a necessary good.
It never explains. It only reveals.

6

The day goes on.
We study what we remember.
We look into the mirror across the room.
We cannot bear to be alone.
The book goes on.
They became silent and did not know how to begin
the dialogue which was necessary.
It was words that created divisions in the first place,
that created loneliness.
They waited.
They would turn the pages, hoping
something would happen.
They would patch up their lives in secret:
each defeat forgiven because it could not be tested,
each pain rewarded because it was unreal.
They did nothing.

7

The book will not survive.
We are the living proof of that.
It is dark outside, in the room it is darker.
I hear your breathing.
You are asking me if I am tired,
if I want to keep reading.
Yes, I am tired.
Yes, I want to keep reading.
I say yes to everything.
You cannot hear me.
They sat beside each other on the couch.
They were the copies, the tired phantoms
of something they had been before.
The attitudes they took were jaded.
They stared into the book
and were horrified by their innocence,
their reluctance to give up.
They sat beside each other on the couch.
They were determined to accept the truth.
Whatever it was they would accept it.
The book would have to be written
and would have to be read.
They are the book and they are
nothing else.

The Untelling

He leaned forward over the paper
and for a long time saw nothing.
Then, slowly, the lake opened
like a white eye
and he was a child
playing with his cousins,
and there was a lawn
and a row of trees
that went to the water.
It was a warm afternoon in August
and there was a party
about to begin.
He leaned forward over the paper
and he wrote:

I waited with my cousins across the lake,
watching the grown-ups walking on the far side
along the bank shaded by elms. It was hot.
The sky was clear. My cousins and I stood
for hours among the heavy branches, watching
our parents, and it seemed as if nothing would enter
their lives to make them change, not even the man
running over the lawn, waving a sheet
of paper and shouting. They moved beyond the claims
of weather, beyond whatever news there was,
and did not see the dark begin to deepen
in the trees and bushes, and rise in the folds
of their own dresses and in the stiff white

of their own shirts. Waves of laughter carried
over the water where we, the children, were watching.
It was a scene that was not ours. We were
too far away, and soon we would leave.

He leaned back.
How could he know
the scene was not his?
The summer was with him,
the voices had returned, and he saw the faces.
The day had started before the party;
it had rained in the morning
and suddenly cleared in time.
The hems of the dresses were wet.
The men's shoes glistened.
There was a cloud shaped like a hand
which kept lowering.
There was no way to know
why there were times that afternoon
the lawn seemed empty, or why even then
the voices of the grown-ups lingered there.
He took what he had written
and put it aside.
He sat down and began again:

We all went down to the lake, over the lawn,
walking, not saying a word. All the way
from the house, along the shade cast by the elms.
And the sun bore down, lifting the dampness, allowing
the lake to shine like a clear plate surrounded
by mist. We sat and stared at the water and then
lay down on the grass and slept. The air turned colder.
The wind shook the trees. We lay so long we imagined

a hand brushing the fallen leaves from our faces.
But it was not autumn, and some of us, the youngest,
got up and went to the other side of the lake
and stared at the men and women asleep; the men
in stiff white shirts, the women in pale dresses.
We watched all afternoon. And a man ran down
from the house, shouting, waving a sheet of paper.
And the sleepers rose as if nothing had happened,
as if the night had not begun to move
into the trees. We heard their laughter, then
their sighs. They lay back down, and the dark came over
the lawn and covered them. As far as we know
they are still there, their arms crossed over their chests,
their stiff clothing creased. We have never been back.

He looked at what he had written.
How far had he come?
And why had it grown dark just then?
And wasn't he alone when he watched the others
lie down on the lawn?
He stared out the window,
hoping the people at the lake,
the lake itself, would fade.
He wanted to move beyond his past.
He thought of the man
running over the lawn who seemed familiar.
He looked at what he had written
and wondered how he had crossed the lake,
and if his cousins went with him.
Had someone called?
Had someone waved goodbye?
What he had written told him nothing.
He put it away and began again:

I waited under the trees in front of the house,
thinking of nothing, watching the sunlight wash
over the roof. I heard nothing, felt
nothing, even when she appeared in a long
yellow dress, pointed white shoes, her hair
drawn back in a tight bun; even when
she took my hand and led me along the row
of tall trees toward the lake where the rest had gathered,
the men in their starched shirts, the women in
their summer dresses, the children watching the water.
Even then, my life seemed far away
as though it were waiting for me to discover it.
She held my hand and led me toward the water.
The hem of her dress was wet. She said nothing
when she left me with my cousins and joined
the others who stood together. I knew by the way
they talked that something would happen, that some of us,
the youngest, would go away that afternoon
and never find their way back. As I walked through the woods
to the other side of the lake, their voices faded
in the breaking of leaves and branches underfoot.
Though I walked away, I had no sense of going.
I sat and watched the scene across the lake,
I watched and did nothing. Small waves of laughter
carried over the water and then died down.
I was not moved. Even when the man
ran across the lawn, shouting, I did nothing.
It seemed as if the wind drew the dark
from the trees onto the grass. The adults stood
together. They would never leave that shore.
I watched the one in the yellow dress whose name
I had begun to forget and who waited with
the others and who stared at where I was

but could not see me. Already the full moon
had risen and dropped its white ashes on the lake.
And the woman and the others slowly began
to take off their clothes, and the mild rushes of wind
rinsed their skin, their pale bodies shone
briefly among the shadows until they lay
on the damp grass. And the children had all gone.
And that was all. And even then I felt
nothing. I knew that I would never see
the woman in the yellow dress again,
and that the scene by the lake would not be repeated,
and that that summer would be a place too distant
for me to find myself in again.
Although I have tried to return, I have always
ended here, where I am now. The lake
still exists, and so does the lawn, though the people
who slept there that afternoon have not been seen since.

It bothered him,
as if too much had been said.
He would have preferred
the lake without a story,
or no story and no lake.
His pursuit was a form of evasion:
the more he tried to uncover
the more there was to conceal
the less he understood.
If he kept it up,
he would lose everything.
He knew this
and remembered what he could—
always at a distance,
on the other side of the lake,

or across the lawn,
always vanishing, always there.
And the woman and the others would save him
and he would save them.
He put his hand on the paper.
He would write a letter for the man
running across the lawn.
He would say what he knew.
He rested his head in his arms and tried to sleep.
He knew that night had once come,
that something had once happened.
He wanted to know but not to know.
Maybe something had happened
one afternoon in August.
Maybe he was there or waiting to be there,
waiting to come running across a lawn
to a lake where people were staring
across the water.
He would come running
and be too late.
The people there would be asleep.
Their children would be watching them.
He would bring what he had written
and then would lie down with the others.
He would be the man
he had become, the man
who would run across the lawn.
He began again:

I sat in the house that looked down on the lake,
the lawn, the woods beside the lawn. I heard
the children near the shore, their voices lifted
where no memory of the place would reach.

I watched the women, the men in white, strolling
in the August heat. I shut the window
and saw them in the quiet glass, passing
each time farther away. The trees began
to darken and the children left. I saw
the distant water fade in the gray shade
of grass and underbrush across the lake.
I thought I saw the children sitting, watching
their parents in a slow parade along
the shore. The shapes among the trees kept changing.
It may have been one child I saw, its face.
It may have been my own face looking back.
I felt myself descend into the future.
I saw beyond the lawn, beyond the lake,
beyond the waiting dark, the end of summer,
the end of autumn, the icy air, the silence,
and then, again, the windowpane. I was
where I was, where I would be, and where I am.
I watched the men and women as the white
eye of the lake began to close and deepen
into blue, then into black. It was too late
for them to call the children. They lay on the grass
and the wind blew and shook the first leaves loose.
I wanted to tell them something. I saw myself
running, waving a sheet of paper, shouting,
telling them all that I had something to give them,
but when I got there, they were gone.

He looked up from the paper
and saw himself in the window.
It was an August night
and he was tired,
and the trees swayed

and the wind shook the window.
It was late.
It did not matter.
He would never catch up
with his past. His life
was slowing down.
It was going.
He could feel it,
could hear it in his speech.
It sounded like nothing,
yet he would pass it on.
And his children would live in it
and they would pass it on,
and it would always sound
like hope dying, like space opening,
like a lawn, or a lake,
or an afternoon.
And pain could not give it
the meaning it lacked;
there was no pain,
only disappearance.
Why had he begun in the first place?
He was tired,
and gave himself up to sleep,
and slept where he was,
and slept without dreaming,
so that when he woke
it seemed as if nothing had happened.
The lake opened like a white eye,
the elms rose over the lawn,
the sun over the elms.
It was as he remembered it—
the mist, the dark, the heat,

the woods on the other side.
He sat for a long time
and saw that they had come
and were on the lawn.
They were waiting for him,
staring up at the window.
The wind blew their hair
and they made no motion.
He was afraid to follow them.
He knew what would happen.
He knew the children would wander off,
that he would lie down with their parents.
And he was afraid.
When they turned
and walked down to the lake
into the shade cast by the elms
the children did wander off.
He saw them in the distance,
across the lake, and wondered if one
would come back someday
and be where he was now.
He saw the adults on the lawn,
beginning to lie down.
And he wanted to warn them,
to tell them what he knew.
He ran from the house down to the lake,
knowing that he would be late,
that he would be left
to continue.
When he got there,
they were gone,
and he was alone in the dark,
unable to speak.

He stood still.
He felt the world recede
into the clouds,
into the shelves of air.
He closed his eyes.
He thought of the lake,
the closets of weeds.
He thought of the moth asleep
in the dust of its wings,
of the bat hanging in the caves of trees.
He felt himself at that moment to be
more than his need to survive,
more than his losses,
because he was less than anything.
He swayed back and forth.
The silence was in him
and it rose like joy,
like the beginning.
When he opened his eyes,
the silence had spread, the sheets
of darkness seemed endless,
the sheets he held in his hand.
He turned and walked to the house.
He went to the room
that looked out on the lawn.
He sat and began to write:

The Untelling

To the Woman in the Yellow Dress

The Monument

To the translator of
The Monument
in the future:
"Siste Viator"

I

Let me introduce myself. I am . . . and so on and so forth. Now you know more about me than I know about you.

2

*I am setting out from the meeting with what I am, with what I now begin to be, my descendant and my ancestor, my father and my son, my unlike likeness.**

Though I am reaching over hundreds of years as if they did not exist, imagining you at this moment trying to imagine me, and proving finally that imagination accomplishes more than history, you know me better than I know you. Maybe my voice is dim as it reaches over so many years, so many that they seem one long blur erased and joined by events and lives that become one event, one life; even so, my voice is sufficient to make The Monument out of this moment.

*Sources for this and all quotations in *The Monument* are listed in the acknowledgments, pp. 133–4.

3

And just as there are areas of our soul which flower and give fruit only beneath the gaze of some spirit come from the eternal region to which they belong in time, just so, when that gaze is hidden from us by absence, these areas long for that magical gaze like the earth longing for the sun so that it may give out flowering plants and fruit.

> *Shine alone, shine nakedly, shine like bronze,*
> *that reflects neither my face nor any inner part*
> *of my being, shine like fire, that mirrors nothing.*

Why have I chosen this way to continue myself under your continuing gaze? I might have had my likeness carved in stone, but it is not my image that I want you to have, nor my life, nor the life around me, only this document. What I include of myself is unreal and distracting. Only this luminous moment has life, this instant in which we both write, this flash of voice.

4

> *Look in thy glass, and tell the face thou viewest*
> *Now is the time that face should form another . . .*

Many would have thought it an Happiness to have had their lot of Life in some notable Conjunctures of Ages past;

but the uncertainty of future Times hath tempted few to make a part in Ages to come.

And the secret of human life, the universal secret, the root secret from which all other secrets spring, is the longing for more life, the furious and insatiable desire to be everything else without ever ceasing to be ourselves, to take possession of the entire universe without letting the universe take possession of us and absorb us; it is the desire to be someone else without ceasing to be myself, and continue being myself at the same time I am someone else . . .

It is a struggle to believe I am writing to someone else, to you, when I imagine the spectral conditions of your existence. This work has allowed you to exist, yet this work exists because you are translating it. Am I wrong? It must be early morning as you write. You sit in a large, barely furnished room with one window from which you can see a gray body of water on which several black ducks are asleep. How still the world is so many years from now. How few people there are. They never leave town, never visit the ruins of the great city.

5

Or let me put it this way. You must imagine that you are the author of this work, that the wind is blowing from the northeast, bringing rain that slaps and spatters against your windows. You must imagine the ocean's swash and backwash sounding hushed and muffled. Imagine a long room with a light at one end, illuminating a desk, a chair, papers. Imagine someone is in the chair. Imagine he is you; it is long ago and you are dressed in the absurd clothes of the time. You must imagine yourself asking the question: which of us has sought the other?

6

I have no rest from myself. I feel as though I am devouring my whole life . . .

O my soul, I gave you all, and I have emptied all my hands to you; and now—now you say to me, smiling and full of melancholy, "Which of us has to be thankful? Should not the giver be thankful that the receiver received? Is not giving a need? Is not receiving a mercy?"

All voice is but echo caught from a soundless voice.

In what language do I live? I live in none. I live in you. It is your voice that I begin to hear and it has no language. I hear the motions of a spirit and the sound of what is secret becomes, for me, a voice that is your voice speaking in my ear. It is a misery unheard of to know the secret has no name, no language I can learn.

7

Oh if you knew! If you knew! How it has been. How the ladies of the house would talk softly in the moonlight under the orange trees of the courtyard, impressing upon me the sweetness of their voices and something mysterious in the quietude of their lives. Oh the heaviness of that air, the perfume of jasmine, pale lights against the stones of the courtyard walls. Monument! Monument! How will you ever know!

8

Then do thy office, Muse; I teach thee how
To make him seem, long hence, as he shows now.

Through you I shall be born again; myself again and again; myself without others; myself with a tomb; myself beyond death. I imagine you taking my name; I imagine you saying *myself myself* again and again. And suddenly there will be no blue sky or sun or shape of anything without that simple utterance.

9

. . . Nothing must stand
Between you and the shapes you take
When the crust of shape has been destroyed.
You as you are? You are yourself.

It has been necessary to submit to vacancy in order to begin again, to clear ground, to make space. I can allow nothing to be received. Therein lies my triumph *and* my mediocrity. Nothing is the destiny of everyone, it is our commonness made dumb. I am passing it on. The Monument is a void, artless and everlasting. What I was I am no longer. I speak for nothing, the nothing that I am, the nothing that is this work. And you shall perpetuate me not in the name of what I was, but in the name of what I am.

10

Perhaps there is no monument and this is invisible writing that has appeared in fate's corridor; you are no mere translator but an interpreter-angel.

11

I begin to sense your impatience. It is hard for you to believe that I am what you were. It is a barren past that I represent—one that would have you be its sole guardian. But consider how often we are given to invent ourselves; maybe once, but even so we say we are another, another entirely similar.

12

Stories are told of people who die and after a moment come back to life, telling of a radiance and deep calm they experienced. I too died once but said nothing until this moment, not wishing to upset my friends or to allow my enemies jokes about whether I was really alive to begin with. It happened a couple of years ago in March or April. I was having coffee. I know I was dead just a few minutes because the coffee was still warm when I came back. I saw no light, felt no radiance. I saw my life flash before me as a succession of meals and I felt full. This feeling was to give way to an image of waste. How much would be lost! A box placed underground with me inside would never be right. And then I thought of The Monument. It was this promise of adequate memorial that brought me back to life, to my room and my coffee.

13

Stars denote places where The Monument has been reported.

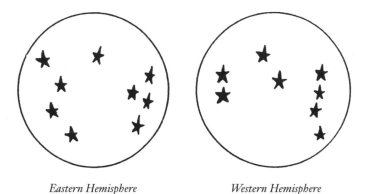

Eastern Hemisphere   *Western Hemisphere*

14

It may be wise at this time to get down to practical matters, to make suggestions that will ease your task. There are words that I use, words used often in the poetry of my day, which should not constrain you. It is possible that they will not exist in your time or in your language. In either case, find words for which you yourself have a fondness. If this is difficult, then I suggest you use one word to cover the many. The objects you see from where you sit may be "anything." "Any-thing" may be "nothing," depending on what your feeling is. If "nothing" conveys the wrong idea, use "something." By all means, use "something" if you agree with the poet who shrieks, "There is not noth-ing, no, no, never nothing."

15

The certainty of death is attended by uncertainties, in time, manner, places. The variety of Monuments hath often ob-scured true graves: and Cenotaphs confounded Sepulchres.

The true Monument must survive, must stand by itself despite the possible survival of false monuments. Do not be taken in by structures that call themselves The Monument and look like this:

THE MONUMENT

    During the night
    a storm broke,
  striking the monument,
    sending it down,
    stone and green
    pieces of bronze,
    onto the lawn.
    Now it lies

among shrubs
and torn limbs
of trees. You scrape
the pieces clean,
cracks and channels
made by rain, you scrub
away the scars, stains,
names painted
on the pedestal.
When you are done,
nothing about
the monument
will look the same.
The cape will gleam,
curls of hair
will seem to swirl
in the moonlight
or spill
in the bright sun.
No wind will scream
under the arms or chin;
all signs and syllables
of pain will be
rephrased, and when
you leave the monument's
hard gaze, the cold
violet of its shade,
you will not think
of turning back.
Not even fears
of slow decay,
of fires blazing
at its base,

will keep you there.
Before you walk away,
you will drop a list
inside its throat
of what to do in case
it falls again.
Your final say
buried in the monument's
cold shape . . .

16

Or look like this:

THE MONUMENT

You will see it
in the shade or covered
with a shawl
of sunlight or sheen
of wet gray;
or later, barely
visible while
the night passes
with its silent cargo
of moons and stars.
You will see sleeping
figures at its feet;
you will see

in its bleached eyes
baked by sun,
strafed by rain,
the meanness of
the sky; and in
its barely open mouth
perpetual twilight.
You will see it
when you come
and when you leave,
you will see it
when you do not wish to
and you will never know
whose monument it is
or why it came to you . . .

17

How sad it is to come back to one's work, so much less than the world it masks or echoes or reminds one of. Such dreariness to return to one's singleness, one's simple reductions. Poems have come to seem so little. Even The Monument is little. How it wishes it were something it cannot be—its own perpetual birth instead of its death again and again, each sentence a memorial.

18

If you want me again look for me under your boot-soles.

Who walks where I am not,
Who remains standing when I die.

The Unmonument is my memorial placed upside down in the earth. This least obtrusive of reminders will disturb no one, being in fact a way of burying my death. The inverse of such a tactic would be the un-burial of my life. That is, so long as my monument is underground, my life shall remain above. Friend, you are my collaborator in this venture. How much plea-sure it gives me to imagine you standing on the very ground that covers my statue, saying:

From south and east and west and north,
roads coming together have led me
to my secret center . . .

And of course it will be late in the day and you will consider the events of your life from the greatest to the most humble. Again words will come to you:

Now I can forget them. I reach my center . . .
my mirror.
Soon I shall know who I am.

19

Spare my bones the fire,
Let me lie entire,
Underground or in the air,
Whichever, I don't care.

Remember the story of my death? Well, I planned it this far in advance. And I did it for you, so you might understand it as none of the others could. When I leaned back on the cold pillows, staring through the open window at the black velvety sky, pointing, though my hand was on the verge of collapsing, and said in a clear, calm voice, "Look! Look!" I was asking the impossible of those loyal friends who were crowded into that small room. For they looked out the window and, seeing nothing, said almost in unison, "What is it?" And I replied in a tone that soothed and urged at once, "There! There!" In a moment I was dead. That is the famous story of my death told, I believe, for a dozen or so years and then forgotten. It is yours because you have found The Monument. Finding The Monument is what I urged when I said, "Look! Look!"

20

It is my belief that on a certain day in a person's life the shapes of all the clouds in the sky will for a single moment directly over his head resemble him. It has been the sad lot of almost everyone who has ever lived to miss this spectacle, but it has not been so with me. Today I saw The Monument affirmed in heaven. I sat in a chair and looked up by chance and this is what I saw:

A story is told of a man who lived his life anticipating his moment in the heavens, and each day there were clouds he would lie on his back in front of his house. He did this summer and winter and the only rest he got was on clear days or days completely overcast. Finally, when he was very old, he did see himself in the clouds and died immediately after. They found him up on his platform, his eyes wide open, the look of astonishment still upon them.

21

We are truly ourselves only when we coincide with nothing, not even ourselves.

Where do I come from? Though unimportant and irrelevant to so single-minded a venture as The Monument, I believe if I included a few paragraphs from an abandoned autobiography you would see for yourself that I am justified in leaving my life out of our work.

I have always said, when speaking of my father's father, Emil, that he died a sudden and tragic death by falling into a giant vat of molten metal. The fact is I know only what my father told me—that he suffered an accident in a steel mill and died. The terseness of my father's explanation (no doubt masking some pain at recalling this stage in his own life) created an impression of mystery and violence in my mind. Since the vat of molten metal was the only image I had of the inside of a steel mill, it actually became for me the sole cause of my grandfather's death. And the horror of it put him in a heroic perspective, a perspective which contributed to my impulse to aggrandize my father. As a small boy I wanted a lineage of heroes. It is significant that I would usually add, as epilogue to the tale of Emil's death, the suggestion that he was now part of a Cleveland skyscraper. There is some primitive irony in this, but also a belief in the ultimate utility of his dying, as though it were not merely an accident but self-sacrifice for the public good. His death has become over the years a myth of origin to which I cling almost unconsciously. I say "almost" because whenever I tell of it I am aware of the slight distortion I may be guilty of. Nevertheless, I feel a compulsion to tell it the way I originally construed it, regardless of the doubts that have increased over the years, and the young boy in me is satisfied.

Of my father's mother, Ida, I have no image what- ever, probably because my father had none either. She died giving birth to him. He weighed fifteen pounds.

22

. . . he ordered them to dig a grave at once, of the right size, and then collect any pieces of marble that they could find and fetch wood and water for the disposal of the corpse. As they bustled about obediently he muttered through his tears: "Dead! And so great an artist!"

It is good none of my enemies, friends, or colleagues has seen this, for they would complain of my narcis- sism as they always seem to, but with—so they would claim—greater cause. They would mistake this mod- est document as self-centered in the extreme, not only because none of their names appears in it, but because I have omitted to mention my wife and daughter. How mistaken they are. This poor document does not have

to do with a self, it dwells on the absence of a self. I—
and this pronoun will have to do—have not permitted
anything worthwhile or memorable to be part of this
communication that strains even to exist in a language
other than the one in which it was written. So much is
excluded that it could not be a document of self-
centeredness. If it is a mirror to anything, it is to the
gap between the nothing that was and the nothing
that will be. It is a thread of longing that binds past
and future. Again, it is everything that history is not.

23

It is easy to lose oneself in nothing because nothing
can interrupt and be unnoticed. Why do I do this?

24

There is a day when the daughters of Necessity sit on
their thrones and chant and souls gather to choose the
next life they will live. After the despots pick beggary,
and the beggars pick wealth, and Orpheus picks swan-
hood, Agamemnon an eagle, Ajax a lion, and Odysseus
the life of quiet obscurity, I come along, pushing my
way through the musical animals, and pick one of the

lots. Since I had no need to compensate for any previous experience and wandered onto that meadow by chance, I found the lot of another man much like me, which is how I found you. And instead of going to the River of Unmindfulness, I wrote this down.

25

The most enclosed being generates waves.

Suppose the worst happens and I am still around while you are reading this? Suppose everybody is around? Well, there is the crystal box!

26

I confess a yearning to make prophetic remarks, to be remembered as someone who was ahead of his time; I would like to be someone about whom future generations would say, as they shifted from foot to foot and stared at the ground, "He knew! He knew!" But I don't know. I know only you, you ahead of my time. I know it is sad, even silly, this longing to say something that will charm or amaze others later on. But one little phrase is all I ask. Friend, say something amazing *for* me. It must be something you take for granted, something meaningless to you, but impossible for me to think of. Say I predicted it. Write it here:

[Translator's note: *Though I wanted to obey the author's request, I could not without violating what I took to be his desire for honesty. I believe he not only wanted it this way, but might have predicted it.*]

27

I am so glad you discovered me. The treatment I have received is appalling. The army of angry poets coming out to whip The Monument.

28

I have begun to mistrust you, my dear friend, and I am sorry. As I proceed with this work, I sense your wish to make it your own. True, I have, in a way, given it to you but it is precisely this spirit of "giving" that must be preserved. You must not "take" what is not really yours. No doubt I am being silly, my fears reflecting jealousy on my part, but I know you only as you work on this text. Whatever else you are is hidden from me.

What I fear is that you will tell people in your day that you made up The Monument, that this is a mock translation, that I am merely a creature of your imagination. I know that I intend this somewhat, but the sweet anonymity and nothingness that I claim as my province *do* cause me pain. As I write I feel that this should not be my memorial, merely, but that it should be passed on in no one's name, not even yours.

29

It occurs to me that you may be a woman. What then? I suppose I become therefore a woman. If you are a woman, I suggest that you curl up inside the belly of The Monument which is buried horizontally in the ground and eventually let yourself out through the mouth. Thus, I can experience, however belatedly, a birth, your birth, the birth of myself as a woman.

30

. . . a Poet's mind
Is labour not unworthy of regard.

And what I say unto you, I say unto all, Watch!

Sometimes when I wander in these woods whose prince I am, I hear a voice and I know that I am not alone. Another voice, another monument becoming one; another tomb, another marker made from elements least visible; another voice that says *Watch it closely.* And I do, and there is someone inside. It is the Bishop, who after all was not intended to be seen. It is the Bishop calling and calling.

31

Such good work as yours should not go unrewarded, so I have written a speech for you, knowing how tired you must be. It should be delivered into the mirror.

> Labors of hate! Labors of love! I can't go on working this way, shedding darkness, shucking light, peeling pages. There is no virtue in it. The author is the opposite of a good author, allowing no people in his work, allowing no plot to carry it forward. Where are the good phrases? They're borrowed! It all adds up to greed—his words in my mouth, his time in my time. He longs to be alive, to continue, yet he says he is nobody. Does he have nothing to say? Probably not. Anonymous, his eyes are fixed upon himself. I grow tired of his jabbering, the freight of his words. My greatest hope is his contin-

ued anonymity, which is why I bother to finish The
Monument.

[Translator's note: *I must say that he has expressed my feeling so
adequately that I find myself admiring him for it and hating myself
somewhat.*]

32

Flotillas! Floating gardens skimming the sky's blue
shell. Great gangs of gang-gangs and galahs. The air
has never been so pure, my lungs are two pink sacks of
moist down-under light. Friend, The Monument
shines in the tabernacle of air, and at night, under the
Southern Cross and the silent sparkling bed of stars, it
sings. Friend, this is the place to do your monument.
Go among the gang-gangs and galahs!

33

The drift of skeletons under the earth, the shifting of
that dark society, those nations of the dead, the
unshaping of their bones into dirt, the night of noth-
ing removing them, turning their absences into the
small zeros of the stars, it is indeed a grave, invisible
workmanship. O Monument, what can be done!

34

They are back, the angry poets. But look! They have come with hammers and little buckets, and they are knocking off pieces of The Monument to study and use in the making of their own small tombs.

35

SONG OF MYSELF

First silence, then some humming,
then more silence, then nothing,
then more nothing, then silence,
then more silence, then nothing.

Song of My Other Self: There is no other self.

The Wind's Song: Get out of my way.

The Sky's Song: You're less than a cloud.

The Tree's Song: You're less than a leaf.

The Sea's Song: You're a wave, less than a wave.

The Sun's Song: You're the moon's child.

The Moon's Song: You're no child of mine.

36

There is a sullen, golden greed in my denials. Yet I wish I were not merely making them up; I wish I could be the lies I tell. This is the truth. Knowledge never helped me sort out anything, and having had no knowledge but of nothing suggests all questions are unanswerable once they are posed. Asking is the act of unresolving, a trope for disclosure.

37

... it is to be remembered, that to raise a Monument is a sober and reflective act; that the inscription which it bears is intended to be permanent and for universal perusal; and that, for this reason, the thoughts and feelings expressed should be permanent also—liberated from that weakness and anguish of sorrow which is in nature transitory, and which with instinctive decency retires from notice. The passions should be subdued, the emotions controlled; strong indeed, but nothing ungovernable or wholly involuntary. Seemliness requires this, and truth requires it also: for how can the Narrator otherwise be trusted?

Julius Scaliger, who in a sleepless Fit of the Gout could make two hundred Verses in a Night, would have but five plain Words upon his Tomb.

Tell me that my ugly tomb, my transcending gesture, my way into the next world, your world, my world made by you, you the future of me, my future, my features translated, tell me that it will improve, that it will seem better for my not giving in to what passes for style, that its prose shall never wear a poem's guise at last, tell me that its perpetual prose will become less than itself and hint always at more.

38

The epic of disbelief
blares oftener and soon . . .

Some will think I wrote this and some will think you wrote this. The fact is neither of us did. There is a ghostly third who has taken up residence in this pen, this pen we hold. Not tangible enough to be described but easy to put a finger on, it is the text already written, unwriting itself into the text of promise. It blooms in its ashes, radiates health in its sickness. It is a new falsity, electric in its clumsiness, glad in its lies. And it loves itself as it fears death.

39

I wonder if my poverty would be more complete without you or whether you complete it, the last straw taken away. Having said such a thing I feel a surge of power, I, a single strand, upright, making translation less and less possible. Beautiful swipes of clarity fall upon me, lights from the luminous bells of heaven. I tell you this robe of harmless flames I wear is no poor man's torn pajamas. There's no poverty here, with or without you. Translate. Translate faster. Brief work, isn't it, this feathery fluke!

40

To be the first of the posthumous poets is to be the oldest. This will make children of the poets of Europe, the dead poets of Europe. There must be something America is first in. Death and postdeath meditations! Glory be! A crown on our heads at last! But what is America to you or you to America?

41

Solemn truths! Lucid inescapable foolishness! None
of that for me! To be the salt of Walt, oceanic in
osteality! Secure in cenotaph! The hysterical herald of
hypogea! The fruit of the tomb! The flute of the
tomb! The loot of gloom! The lute of loot! The work
of soon, of never and ever! Saver of naught. Naughti-
ness of severance. Hoot of hiddenness. I give you my
graven grave, my wordy ossuary, telltale trinket of
transcendence, bauble of babble, tower of tripe, trap
of tribute, thought-taxi from one day to the next, nou-
gat of nothing, germ of gemini, humble hypogeum!

42

We have come to terms without terms, come round
almost to the end. A relief, but only a stage, bare stage,
first stage. We have allowed the enormous airs of the
future to engulf us—to be sung, to be borne and born.
Heirs of ourselves, ourselves heirs, salvos of air. With-
out weight the future is possible, here without our
waiting. I embrace you in this madness, this muscular
mouthing of possibles. The enormous airs—the giant
cloudsongs that will reign and reign. Friend, they are
coming and only we know it. Perhaps we should be
silent, tell no one and the airs will pass, pass without
knowledge of themselves, never having been termed,
tuned in turmoil, termed harmless.

43

Heavy glory upon us. Hang on. I must praise my brothers and sisters in the lost art, spitting into the wind, beating their heads against the stars, eating their words, putting their feet in their mouths, hating each other, all of them either lovely or fearful.

44

I feel nostalgia for poetry and believe The Monument should have some lines like:

> Invisible lords among the stars
> Over the heads of deep astronomers

or:

> The moon sucking the sea, sucking
> The light from our eyes as we sleep

That sort of thing. But it would never do. Too hard to translate out of the original. After the blazing plainness of The Monument's prose it doesn't stand up. And yet, there's a longing that has no voice and wants one, that fears it will die of itself. There are moments that crave memorial as if they were worthy, as if they were history and not merely in it, moments of the bluest sky, of the most intense sun, of the greatest happiness of the least known man or woman, moments that may have gone on for years in the most remote village on earth. They shall exist outside The Monument.

45

We are the enemies of pastoral violence, lovers of cold; the body recumbent like The Monument is for us the goodest good; heavy allusions to weather are just another load to us. Give us a good cigar, a long ash that we can speculate on. And plenty of smoke. Ho hum. Now give us a glass of Spanish brandy. Give us a blank wall that we might see ourselves more truly and more strange. Now give us the paper, the daily paper on which to write. Now give us the day, this day. Take it away. The space that is left is The Monument.

46

It is the crystal box again. Let it be a sunlit tomb, a clear tumulus. Let us stand by it, by the life it promises. If we bask in its brightness, we shall be saved, we shall grow into the language that calls from the future, The Monument reaching out.

47

Spin out from your entrails, therefore, my soul, and let come what may! More empty space, more void . . .

> *Till the bridge you will need be form'd,*
>   *till the ductile anchor hold.*
> *Till the gossamer thread you fling catch*
>   *somewhere, O my soul.*

Prose is the language of meaning so I suppose I mean what I say. I say what I say because it is prose. And so it is; describing the circle, the naught of my means, I am taking away, subtracting myself from my words. My blank prose travels into the future, its freight the fullness of zero, the circumference of absence. And it misses something, something I remember I wanted. Soon I shall disappear into the well of want, the *lux* of lack.

48

It is the giant of nothingness that rises beyond, that rises beyond beyondness, undiscovered in the vault of the future, in the leap of faith. If there were a limb here, a limb there, on the desert sand, *that* would be something. If on the pedestal these words appeared, "I am The Monument. Should you doubt this, look around you and compare," *that* would be something. But The Monument has no monument. There are no powers that will work for it; earth, sky, and breathing of the common air, all will forget. O most unhappy Monument! The giant of nothingness rising in sleep like the beginning of language, like language being born into the sleeper's future, his dream of himself entering the beyond. O happy Monument! The giant of nothing is taking you with him!

49

I have no apologies, no words for disbelievers. What do I care if there is nothing sublime in this summery encounter with the void or voided mirror? We go our ways, each without the other, going without a theory of direction, going because we have to. Why make excuses? Friend, tell them I see myself only as happy. Let them say what they will, The Monument will pretend to be dead.

50

Here I lie dead, and here I wait for thee:
So thou shalt wait
Soon for some other; since all mortals be
Bound to one fate.

Our Fathers finde their graves in our short memories, and sadly tell us how we may be buried in our Survivors.

Now here I am at the end waiting for you, ahead of my time, ahead of yours. Such irony should be its own reward, but here I am at the end, the letter ended, The Monument concluded, but only briefly; for it must continue, must gather its words and send them off into another future, your future, my future. O poor Monument to offer so little even to those who have made you!

51

If I were to die now without The Monument, none of my words would remain. How sad it is to think of the hours wasted while this triumph of ease and crudity that has taken so little time should last centuries, towering over the corpses of poems whose lyrical natures flew off like the best intentions. If I were to die now, I would change my name so it might appear that the author of my works were still alive. No I wouldn't. If I were to die now, it would be only a joke, a cruel joke played on fortune. If I were to die now, your greatest work would remain forever undone. My last words would be *Don't finish it.*

52

. . . Oh, how do I bear to go on living! And how could I bear
to die now!

> *O living always, always dying!*
> *O the burials of me past and present,*
> *O me while I stride ahead, material, visible,*
>   *imperious as ever;*
> *O me, what I was for years, now dead, (I lament not,*
>   *I am content;)*
> *O to disengage myself from those corpses of me,*
>   *which I turn and look at where I cast them,*
> *To pass on, (O living! always living!) and leave the*
>   *corpses behind.*

ACKNOWLEDGMENTS

Sources of the quotations used in The Monument *are listed here by section and in the order in which they appear in each section.*

2 "The Old Poem" by Octavio Paz. From *Eagle or Sun?*, translated by Eliot Weinberger. Copyright © 1976 by Octavio Paz and Eliot Weinberger. Reprinted by permission of New Directions Publishing Corporation.

3 "The Secret of Life" by Miguel de Unamuno. From *The Agony of Christianity and Essays on Faith*, translated by Anthony Kerrigan. Copyright © 1974 by Princeton University Press. Volume 5 of *The Selected Works of Miguel de Unamuno*, Bollingen Series LXXXV. Reprinted with permission of Princeton University Press.
"Nuances of a Theme by Williams" by Wallace Stevens. From *The Collected Poems of Wallace Stevens*. Copyright © 1954 by Wallace Stevens. Reprinted by permission of Alfred A. Knopf, a division of Random House, Inc.

4 Sonnet Number 3 by William Shakespeare.
"Letter to a Friend" by Sir Thomas Browne. From *The Prose of Sir Thomas Browne*, edited by Norman Endicott and Kathleen Endicott (Doubleday, a division of Random House, Inc., New York).
"The Secret of Life" by Miguel de Unamuno, translated by Anthony Kerrigan. Copyright © 1974 by Princeton University Press. Volume 5 of *The Selected Works of Miguel de Unamuno*, Bollingen Series LXXXV. Reprinted with permission of Princeton University Press.

6 *The Seagull* by Anton Chekhov. *Thus Spoke Zarathustra* by Friedrich Nietzsche.
"Colder Fire" by Robert Penn Warren. From *Selected Poems 1923–1975*. Copyright © 1955 by Robert Penn Warren. Reprinted by permission of Random House, Inc.

8 Sonnet Number 101 by William Shakespeare.

9 "The Man with the Blue Guitar" by Wallace Stevens. From *The Collected Poems of Wallace Stevens*. Copyright © 1954 by Wallace Stevens. Reprinted by permission of Alfred A. Knopf, a division of Random House, Inc.

15 "Hydriotaphia or Urne Buriall" by Sir Thomas Browne. From *The Prose of Sir Thomas Browne*, edited by Norman Endicott and Kathleen Endicott (Doubleday, a division of Random House, Inc., New York).

18 "Song of Myself" by Walt Whitman.
"I Am Not I" by Juan Ramón Jiménez. From *Lorca and Jiménez: Selected Poems*, translated by Robert Bly (Beacon Press, Boston, 1973). Copyright © 1973 by Robert Bly. Reprinted by permission of Robert Bly.
In Praise of Darkenss by Jorge Luis Borges, translated by Norman Thomas di Giovanni. Copyright © 1969, 1970, 1971, 1972, 1973, 1974 by Emece Editores S.A.

From *The Late Hour*

The Coming of Light

Even this late it happens:
the coming of love, the coming of light.
You wake and the candles are lit as if by themselves,
stars gather, dreams pour into your pillows,
sending up warm bouquets of air.
Even this late the bones of the body shine
and tomorrow's dust flares into breath.

Another Place

I walk
into what light
there is

not enough for blindness
or clear sight
of what is to come

yet I see
the water
the single boat
the man standing

he is not someone I know

this is another place
what light there is
spreads like a net
over nothing

what is to come
has come to this
before

this is the mirror
in which pain is asleep
this is the country
nobody visits

Lines for Winter

Tell yourself
as it gets cold and gray falls from the air
that you will go on
walking, hearing
the same tune no matter where
you find yourself—
inside the dome of dark
or under the cracking white
of the moon's gaze in a valley of snow.
Tonight as it gets cold
tell yourself
what you know which is nothing
but the tune your bones play
as you keep going. And you will be able
for once to lie down under the small fire
of winter stars.
And if it happens that you cannot
go on or turn back
and you find yourself
where you will be at the end,
tell yourself
in that final flowing of cold through your limbs
that you love what you are.

My Son

(after Carlos Drummond de Andrade)

My son
my only son,
the one I never had,
would be a man today.

He moves
in the wind,
fleshless, nameless.
Sometimes

he comes
and leans his head,
lighter than air
against my shoulder

and I ask him,
Son,
where do you stay,
where do you hide?

And he answers me
with a cold breath,
You never noticed
though I called

and called
and keep on calling
from a place
beyond,

beyond love,
where nothing,
everything,
wants to be born.

For Jessica, My Daughter

Tonight I walked,
close to the house,
and was afraid,
not of the winding course
that I have made of love and self
but of the dark and faraway.
I walked, hearing the wind
and feeling the cold,
but what I dwelled on
were the stars blazing
in the immense arc of sky.

Jessica, it is so much easier
to think of our lives,
as we move under the brief luster of leaves,
loving what we have,
than to think of how it is
such small beings as we
travel in the dark
with no visible way
or end in sight.

Yet there were times I remember
under the same sky
when the body's bones became light
and the wound of the skull
opened to receive
the cold rays of the cosmos,

and were, for an instant,
themselves the cosmos,
there were times when I could believe
we were the children of stars
and our words were made of the same
dust that flames in space,
times when I could feel in the lightness of breath
the weight of a whole day
come to rest.

But tonight
it is different.
Afraid of the dark
in which we drift or vanish altogether,
I imagine a light
that would not let us stray too far apart,
a secret moon or mirror,
a sheet of paper,
something you could carry
in the dark
when I am away.

From The Long Sad Party

Someone was saying
something about shadows covering the field, about
how things pass, how one sleeps toward morning
and the morning goes.

Someone was saying
how the wind dies down but comes back,
how shells are the coffins of wind
but the weather continues.

It was a long night
and someone said something about the moon shedding its white
on the cold field, that there was nothing ahead
but more of the same.

Someone mentioned
a city she had been in before the war, a room with two candles
against a wall, someone dancing, someone watching.
We began to believe

the night would not end.
Someone was saying the music was over and no one had noticed.
Then someone said something about the planets, about the stars,
how small they were, how far away.

The Late Hour

A man walks toward town,
a slack breeze smelling of earth
and the raw green of trees blows at his back.

He drags the weight of his passion as if nothing were over,
as if the woman, now curled in bed beside her lover,
still cared for him.

She is awake and stares at scars of light
trapped in the panes of glass.
He stands under her window, calling her name;

he calls all night and it makes no difference.
It will happen again, he will come back wherever she is.
Again he will stand outside and imagine

her eyes opening in the dark
and see her rise to the window and peer down.
Again she will lie awake beside her lover

and hear the voice from somewhere in the dark.
Again the late hour, the moon and stars,
the wounds of night that heal without sound,

again the luminous wind of morning that comes before the sun.
And, finally, without warning or desire,
the lonely and the feckless end.

The Story

It is the old story: complaints about the moon
sinking into the sea, about stars in the first light fading,
about the lawn wet with dew, the lawn silver, the lawn cold.

It goes on and on: a man stares at his shadow
and says it's the ash of himself falling away, says his days
are the real black holes in space. But none of it's true.

You know the one I mean: it's the one about the minutes dying,
and the hours, and the years; it's the story I tell
about myself, about you, about everyone.

For Her

Let it be anywhere
on any night you wish,
in your room that is empty and dark

or down the street
or at those dim frontiers
you barely see, barely dream of.

You will not feel desire,
nothing will warn you,
no sudden wind, no stillness of air.

She will appear,
looking like someone you knew:
the friend who wasted her life,

the girl who sat under the palm tree.
Her bracelets will glitter,
becoming the lights

of a village you turned from years ago.

So You Say

It is all in the mind, you say, and has
nothing to do with happiness. The coming of cold,
the coming of heat, the mind has all the time in the world.
You take my arm and say something will happen,
something unusual for which we were always prepared,
like the sun arriving after a day in Asia,
like the moon departing after a night with us.

Poor North

It is cold, the snow is deep,
the wind beats around in its cage of trees,
clouds have the look of rags torn and soiled with use,
and starlings peck at the ice.
It is north, poor north. Nothing goes right.

The man of the house has gone to work,
selling chairs and sofas in a failing store.
His wife stays home and stares from the window into the trees,
trying to recall the life she lost, though it wasn't much.
White flowers of frost build up on the glass.

It is late in the day. Brants and Canada geese are asleep
on the waters of St. Margaret's Bay.
The man and his wife are out for a walk; see how they lean
into the wind; they turn up their collars
and the small puffs of their breath are carried away.

Pot Roast

I gaze upon the roast,
that is sliced and laid out
on my plate,
and over it
I spoon the juices
of carrot and onion.
And for once I do not regret
the passage of time.

I sit by a window
that looks
on the soot-stained brick of buildings
and do not care that I see
no living thing—not a bird,
not a branch in bloom,
not a soul moving
in the rooms
behind the dark panes.
These days when there is little
to love or to praise
one could do worse
than yield
to the power of food.
So I bend

to inhale
the steam that rises
from my plate, and I think

of the first time
I tasted a roast
like this.
It was years ago
in Seabright,
Nova Scotia;
my mother leaned
over my dish and filled it
and when I finished
filled it again.
I remember the gravy,
its odor of garlic and celery,
and sopping it up
with pieces of bread.

And now
I taste it again.
The meat of memory.
The meat of no change.
I raise my fork
and I eat.

The House in French Village

for Elizabeth Bishop

It stood by itself
in a sloping field,
it was white
with green
shutters and trim,

and its gambrel roof
gave it the look
of a small
prim barn.
From the porch

when the weather was clear,
I could see Fox Point,
across the bay
where the fishermen,
I was told,

laid out
their catch of tuna
on the pier
and hacked away with axes
at the bellies

of the giant fish.
I would stare
at Wedge Island
where gulls wheeled
in loud broken rings

above their young;
at Albert Hubley's shack
built over water, and sagging;
at Boutelier's wharf
loaded down

with barrels of brine
and nets to be mended.
I would sit
with my grandmother,
my aunt, and my mother,

the four of us rocking
on chairs, watching
the narrow dirt road
for a sign
of the black

baby Austin
my father would drive
to town and back.
But the weather
was not often clear

and all we could see
were sheets of cold rain
sweeping this way and that,
riffling the sea's coat
of deep green,

and the wind
beating the field flat,
sending up to the porch

gusts of salt spray
that carried

the odor of fish
and the rot,
so it seemed,
of the whole bay,
while we kept watch.

The Garden

for Robert Penn Warren

It shines in the garden,
in the white foliage of the chestnut tree,
in the brim of my father's hat
as he walks on the gravel.

In the garden suspended in time
my mother sits in a redwood chair;
light fills the sky,
the folds of her dress,
the roses tangled beside her.

And when my father bends
to whisper in her ear,
when they rise to leave
and the swallows dart
and the moon and stars
have drifted off together, it shines.

Even as you lean over this page,
late and alone, it shines; even now
in the moment before it disappears.

Snowfall

Watching snow cover the ground, cover itself,
cover everything that is not you, you see
it is the downward drift of light
upon the sound of air sweeping away the air,
it is the fall of moments into moments, the burial
of sleep, the down of winter, the negative of night.

From *Selected Poems*

Shooting Whales

for Judith and Leon Major

When the shoals of plankton
swarmed into St. Margaret's Bay,
turning the beaches pink,
we saw from our place on the hill
the sperm whales feeding,
fouling the nets
in their play,
and breaching clean
so the humps of their backs
rose over the wide sea meadows.

Day after day
we waited inside
for the rotting plankton to disappear.
The smell stilled even the wind,
and the oxen looked stunned,
pulling hay on the slope
of our hill.
But the plankton kept coming in
and the whales would not go.

That's when the shooting began.
The fishermen got in their boats
and went after the whales,
and my father and uncle
and we children went, too.
The froth of our wake sank fast
in the wind-shaken water.

159

The whales surfaced close by.
Their foreheads were huge,
the doors of their faces were closed.
Before sounding, they lifted
their flukes into the air
and brought them down hard.
They beat the sea into foam,
and the path that they made
shone after them.

Though I did not see their eyes,
I imagined they were
like the eyes of mourning,
glazed with rheum,
watching us, sweeping along
under the darkening sheets of salt.

When we cut our engine and waited
for the whales to surface again,
the sun was setting,
turning the rock-strewn barrens a gaudy salmon.
A cold wind flailed at our skin.
When finally the sun went down
and it seemed like the whales had gone,
my uncle, no longer afraid,
shot aimlessly into the sky.

Three miles out
in the rolling dark
under the moon's astonished eyes,
our engine would not start
and we headed home in the dinghy.
And my father, hunched over the oars,

brought us in. I watched him,
rapt in his effort, rowing against the tide,
his blond hair glistening with salt.
I saw the slick spillage of moonlight
being blown over his shoulders,
and the sea and spindrift
suddenly silver.

He did not speak the entire way.

At midnight
when I went to bed,
I imagined the whales
moving beneath me,
sliding over the weed-covered hills of the deep;
they knew where I was;
they were luring me
downward and downward
into the murmurous
waters of sleep.

Nights in Hackett's Cove

Those nights lit by the moon and the moon's nimbus,
the bones of the wrecked pier rose crooked in air
and the sea wore a tarnished coat of silver.
The black pines waited. The cold air smelled
of fishheads rotting under the pier at low tide.
The moon kept shedding its silver clothes
over the bogs and pockets of bracken.
Those nights I would gaze at the bay road,
at the cottages clustered under the moon's immaculate stare,
nothing hinted that I would suffer so late
this turning away, this longing to be there.

A Morning

I have carried it with me each day: that morning I took
my uncle's boat from the brown water cove
and headed for Mosher Island.
Small waves splashed against the hull
and the hollow creak of oarlock and oar
rose into the woods of black pine crusted with lichen.
I moved like a dark star, drifting over the drowned
other half of the world until, by a distant prompting,
I looked over the gunwale and saw beneath the surface
a luminous room, a light-filled grave, saw for the first time
the one clear place given to us when we are alone.

My Mother on an Evening in Late Summer

1

When the moon appears
and a few wind-stricken barns stand out
in the low-domed hills
and shine with a light
that is veiled and dust-filled
and that floats upon the fields,
my mother, with her hair in a bun,
her face in shadow, and the smoke
from her cigarette coiling close
to the faint yellow sheen of her dress,
stands near the house
and watches the seepage of late light
down through the sedges,
the last gray islands of cloud
taken from view, and the wind
ruffling the moon's ash-colored coat
on the black bay.

2

Soon the house, with its shades drawn closed, will send
small carpets of lampglow
into the haze and the bay
will begin its loud heaving
and the pines, frayed finials
climbing the hill, will seem to graze

the dim cinders of heaven.
And my mother will stare into the starlanes,
the endless tunnels of nothing,
and as she gazes,
under the hour's spell,
she will think how we yield each night
to the soundless storms of decay
that tear at the folding flesh,
and she will not know
why she is here
or what she is prisoner of
if not the conditions of love that brought her to this.

3

My mother will go indoors
and the fields, the bare stones,
will drift in peace, small creatures—
the mouse and the swift—will sleep
at opposite ends of the house.
Only the cricket will be up,
repeating its one shrill note
to the rotten boards of the porch,
to the rusted screens, to the air, to the rimless dark,
to the sea that keeps to itself.
Why should my mother awake?
The earth is not yet a garden
about to be turned. The stars
are not yet bells that ring
at night for the lost.
It is much too late.

From *The Continuous Life*

The Idea

for Nolan Miller

For us, too, there was a wish to possess
Something beyond the world we knew, beyond ourselves,
Beyond our power to imagine, something nevertheless
In which we might see ourselves; and this desire
Came always in passing, in waning light, and in such cold
That ice on the valley's lakes cracked and rolled,
And blowing snow covered what earth we saw,
And scenes from the past, when they surfaced again,
Looked not as they had, but ghostly and white
Among false curves and hidden erasures;
And never once did we feel we were close
Until the night wind said, "Why do this,
Especially now? Go back to the place you belong";
And there appeared, with its windows glowing, small,
In the distance, in the frozen reaches, a cabin;
And we stood before it, amazed at its being there,
And would have gone forward and opened the door,
And stepped into the glow and warmed ourselves there,
But that it was ours by not being ours,
And should remain empty. That was the idea.

Velocity Meadows

I can say now that nothing was possible
But leaving the house and standing in front of it, staring
As long as I could into the valley. I knew that a train,
Trailing a scarf of smoke, would arrive, that soon it would rain.
A frieze of clouds lowered a shadow over the town,
And a driving wind flattened the meadows that swept
Beyond the olive trees and banks of hollyhock and rose.
The air smelled sweet, and a girl was waving a stick
At some crows so far away they seemed like flies.
Her mother, wearing a cape and shawl, shielded her eyes.
I wondered from what, since there was no sun. Then someone
Appeared and said, "Look at those clouds forming a wall, those crows
Falling out of the sky, those fields, pale green, green-yellow,
Rolling away, and that girl and her mother, waving goodbye."
In a moment the sky was stained with a reddish haze,
And the person beside me was running away. It was dusk,
The lights of the town were coming on, and I saw, dimly at first,
Close to the graveyard bound by rows of cypress bending down,
The girl and her mother, next to each other,
Smoking, grinding their heels into the ground.

A.M.

for Lee Rust Brown

. . . And here the dark infinitive to feel,
Which would endure and have the earth be still
And the star-strewn night pour down the mountains
Into the hissing fields and silent towns until the last
Insomniac turned in, must end, and early risers see
The scarlet clouds break up and golden plumes of smoke
From uniform dark homes turn white, and so on down
To the smallest blade of grass and fallen leaf
Touched by the arriving light. Another day has come,
Another fabulous escape from the damages of night,
So even the gulls, in the ragged circle of their flight,
Above the sea's long lanes that flash and fall, scream
Their approval. How well the sun's rays probe
The rotting carcass of a skate, how well
They show the worms and swarming flies at work,
How well they shine upon the fatal sprawl
Of everything on earth. How well they love us all

Orpheus Alone

It was an adventure much could be made of: a walk
On the shores of the darkest known river,
Among the hooded, shoving crowds, by steaming rocks
And rows of ruined huts half buried in the muck;
Then to the great court with its marble yard
Whose emptiness gave him the creeps, and to sit there
In the sunken silence of the place and speak
Of what he had lost, what he still possessed of his loss,
And, then, pulling out all the stops, describing her eyes,
Her forehead where the golden light of evening spread,
The curve of her neck, the slope of her shoulders, everything
Down to her thighs and calves, letting the words come,
As if lifted from sleep, to drift upstream,
Against the water's will, where all the condemned
And pointless labor, stunned by his voice's cadence,
Would come to a halt, and even the crazed, disheveled
Furies, for the first time, would weep, and the soot-filled
Air would clear just enough for her, the lost bride,
To step through the image of herself and be seen in the light.
As everyone knows, this was the first great poem,
Which was followed by days of sitting around
In the houses of friends, with his head back, his eyes
Closed, trying to will her return, but finding
Only himself, again and again, trapped
In the chill of his loss, and, finally,
Without a word, taking off to wander the hills
Outside of town, where he stayed until he had shaken

The image of love and put in its place the world
As he wished it would be, urging its shape and measure
Into speech of such newness that the world was swayed,
And trees suddenly appeared in the bare place
Where he spoke and lifted their limbs and swept
The tender grass with the gowns of their shade,
And stones, weightless for once, came and set themselves
    there,
And small animals lay in the miraculous fields of grain
And aisles of corn, and slept. The voice of light
Had come forth from the body of fire, and each thing
Rose from its depths and shone as it never had.
And that was the second great poem,
Which no one recalls anymore. The third and greatest
Came into the world as the world, out of the unsayable,
Invisible source of all longing to be; it came
As things come that will perish, to be seen or heard
Awhile, like the coating of frost or the movement
Of wind, and then no more; it came in the middle of sleep
Like a door to the infinite, and, circled by flame,
Came again at the moment of waking, and, sometimes,
Remote and small, it came as a vision with trees
By a weaving stream, brushing the bank
With their violet shade, with somebody's limbs
Scattered among the matted, mildewed leaves nearby,
With his severed head rolling under the waves,
Breaking the shifting columns of light into a swirl
Of slivers and flecks; it came in a language
Untouched by pity, in lines, lavish and dark,
Where death is reborn and sent into the world as a gift,
So the future, with no voice of its own, nor hope
Of ever becoming more than it will be, might mourn.

Fiction

I think of the innocent lives
Of people in novels who know they'll die
But not that the novel will end. How different they are
From us. Here, the moon stares dumbly down,
Through scattered clouds, onto the sleeping town,
And the wind rounds up the fallen leaves,
And somebody—namely me—deep in his chair,
Riffles the pages left, knowing there's not
Much time for the man and woman in the rented room,
For the red light over the door, for the iris
Tossing its shadow against the wall; not much time
For the soldiers under the trees that line
The river, for the wounded being hauled away
To the cities of the interior where they will stay;
The war that raged for years will come to a close,
And so will everything else, except for a presence
Hard to define, a trace, like the scent of grass
After a night of rain or the remains of a voice
That lets us know without spelling it out
Not to despair; if the end is come, it too will pass.

Luminism

And though it was brief, and slight, and nothing
To have been held on to so long, I remember it,
As if it had come from within, one of the scenes
The mind sets for itself, night after night, only
To part from, quickly and without warning. Sunlight
Flooded the valley floor and blazed on the town's
Westward-facing windows. The streets shimmered like rivers,
And trees, bushes, and clouds were caught in the spill,
And nothing was spared, not the couch we sat on,
Nor the rugs, nor our friends, staring off into space.
Everything drowned in the golden fire. Then Philip
Put down his glass and said: "This hand is just one
In an infinite series of hands. Imagine."
And that was it. The evening dimmed and darkened
Until the western rim of the sky took on
The purple look of a bruise, and everyone stood
And said what a great sunset it had been. This was a while ago,
And it was remarkable, but something else happened then—
A cry, almost beyond our hearing, rose and rose,
As if across time, to touch us as nothing else would,
And so lightly we might live out our lives and not know.
I had no idea what it meant until now.

Life in the Valley

Like many brilliant notions—easy to understand
But hard to believe—the one about our hating it here
Was put aside and then forgot. Those freakish winds
Over the flaming lake, bearing down, bringing a bright
Electrical dust, an ashen air crowded with leaves—
Fallen, ghostly—shading the valley, filling it with
A rushing sound, were not enough to drive us out.
Nor were those times the faded winter sun
Lowered a frozen half-light over the canyons
And silent storms buried the high resorts
With heavy snows. We simply stayed indoors.
Our friends would say the views—starlight over
The clustered domes and towers, the frigid moon
In the water's glass—were great. And we agreed,
And got to like the sight of iron horses rusting
In the fields, and birds with wings outspread,
Their silver bones glowing at the water's edge,
And far away, huge banks of cloud motionless as lead.

The Continuous Life

What of the neighborhood homes awash
In a silver light, of children hunched in the bushes,
Watching the grown-ups for signs of surrender,
Signs that the irregular pleasures of moving
From day to day, of being adrift on the swell of duty,
Have run their course? O parents, confess
To your little ones the night is a long way off
And your taste for the mundane grows; tell them
Your worship of household chores has barely begun;
Describe the beauty of shovels and rakes, brooms and mops;
Say there will always be cooking and cleaning to do,
That one thing leads to another, which leads to another;
Explain that you live between two great darks, the first
With an ending, the second without one, that the luckiest
Thing is having been born, that you live in a blur
Of hours and days, months and years, and believe
It has meaning, despite the occasional fear
You are slipping away with nothing completed, nothing
To prove you existed. Tell the children to come inside,
That your search goes on for something you lost—a name,
A family album that fell from its own small matter
Into another, a piece of the dark that might have been yours,
You don't really know. Say that each of you tries
To keep busy, learning to lean down close and hear
The careless breathing of earth and feel its available
Languor come over you, wave after wave, sending
Small tremors of love through your brief,
Undeniable selves, into your days, and beyond.

Always

for Charles Simic

Always so late in the day
In their rumpled clothes, sitting
Around a table lit by a single bulb,
The great forgetters were hard at work.
They tilted their heads to one side, closing their eyes.
Then a house disappeared, and a man in his yard
With all his flowers in a row.
The great forgetters wrinkled their brows.
Then Florida went and San Francisco
Where tugs and barges leave
Small gleaming scars across the Bay.
One of the great forgetters struck a match.
Gone were the harps of beaded lights
That vault the rivers of New York.
Another filled his glass
And that was it for crowds at evening
Under sulfur-yellow streetlamps coming on.
And afterward Bulgaria was gone, and then Japan.
"Where will it stop?" one of them said.
"Such difficult work, pursuing the fate
Of everything known," said another.
"Down to the last stone," said a third,
"And only the cold zero of perfection
Left for the imagination." And gone
Were North and South America,
And gone as well the moon.
Another yawned, another gazed at the window:
No grass, no trees . . .
The blaze of promise everywhere.

Se la vita è sventura . . . ?

for Charles Wright

Where was it written that today
I would go to the window and, because it was summer,
Imagine warm air filling the high floating rooms of trees
With the odors of grass and tar, that two crazed bees
Would chase each other around in the shade, that a wall
Of storm clouds would rise in the east,
That today of all days a man out walking would catch his breath
And lean his head back, letting the gilded light
Slide over his upturned face, and that a stranger
Appearing from nowhere, suddenly baring a knife,
Would rip him open from belly to sternum, making his moment
In front of my house his last? Where was it written
That the world, because it was merciful after all, would part
To make room for the blurred shape of the murderer
Fleeing the scene, while the victim, who had already
Slipped to his knees, would feel the heat of his whole being pass
Into a brief, translucent cloud unraveling as it was formed?
Or that a sightless gaze would replace his look of amazement,
That, despite what I guessed was his will to survive, to enter
Once more the unreachable sphere of light, he would continue
To fall, and the neighbors, who had gathered by now,
Would peer into his body's dark and watch him sinking
Into his wound like a fly or a mote, becoming
An infinitesimal part of the night, where the drift
Of dreams and the ruins of stars, having the same fate,
Obeying the same rules, in their descent, are alike?
Where was it written that such a night would spread,
Darkly inscribing itself everywhere, or for that matter, where

Was it written that I would be born into myself again and again,
As I am even now, as everything is at this moment,
And feel the fall of flesh into time, and feel it turn,
Soundlessly, slowly, as if righting itself, into line?

One Winter Night

I showed up at a party of Hollywood stars
Who milled about, quoted their memoirs, and drank.
The prettiest one stepped out of her dress, fell
To her knees, and said that only her husband had glimpsed
The shadowy flower of her pudendum, and he was a prince.
A slip of sunlight rode the swell of her breasts
Into the blinding links of her necklace, and crashed.
Out on the lawn, The Platters were singing "Twilight Time."
"Heavenly shades of night are falling . . ." This was a dream.

Later, I went to the window and gazed at a bull, huge and pink,
In a field of snow. Moonlight poured down his back, and the damp
Of his breath spread until he was wreathed in a silver steam.
When he lifted his head, he loosed a bellow that broke and rolled
Like thunder in the rooms below. This, too, was a dream.

The History of Poetry

Our masters are gone and if they returned
Who among us would hear them, who would know
The bodily sound of heaven or the heavenly sound
Of the body, endless and vanishing, that tuned
Our days before the wheeling stars
Were stripped of power? The answer is
None of us here. And what does it mean if we see
The moon-glazed mountains and the town with its silent doors
And water towers, and feel like raising our voices
Just a little, or sometimes during late autumn
When the evening flowers a moment over the western range
And we imagine angels rushing down the air's cold steps
To wish us well, if we have lost our will,
And do nothing but doze, half hearing the sighs
Of this or that breeze drift aimlessly over the failed farms
And wasted gardens? These days when we waken,
Everything shines with the same blue light
That filled our sleep moments before,
So we do nothing but count the trees, the clouds,
The few birds left; then we decide that we shouldn't
Be hard on ourselves, that the past was no better
Than now, for hasn't the enemy always existed,
And wasn't the church of the world already in ruins?

The Continental College of Beauty

When the Continental College of Beauty opened its doors
We looked down hallways covered with old masters
And into rooms where naked figures lounged on marble floors.
And we were moved, but not enough to stay. We hurried on
Until we reached a courtyard overgrown with weeds.
This moved us, too, but in a moment we were nodding off.
The sun was coming up, a violet haze was lifting from the sea,
Coastal hills were turning red, and several people on the beach
Went up in flames. This was the start of something new.
The flames died down. The sun continued on its way.
And lakes inland, in the first light, flashed their scales,
And mountains cast a blue, cold shade on valley floors,
And distant towns awoke . . . this is what we'd waited for.
How quickly the great unfinished world came into view
When the Continental College of Beauty opened its doors.

The Midnight Club

The gifted have told us for years that they want to be loved
For what they are, that they, in whatever fullness is theirs,
Are perishable in twilight, just like us. So they work all night
In rooms that are cold and webbed with the moon's light;
Sometimes, during the day, they lean on their cars,
And stare into the blistering valley, glassy and golden,
But mainly they sit, hunched in the dark, feet on the floor,
Hands on the table, shirts with a bloodstain over the heart.

The Famous Scene

The polished scarlets of sunset sink as failure
Darkens the famous scene: nature's portrait of us
On the shore while the flooding sun soils the palms
And wooden walks before the rows of tiny summer homes.
Oh, and the silent birds are hunched in the trees
Or waiting under the eaves, and over there a boat
Cuts through the swell, releasing its coils of steam.
What does it mean to have come here so late?
Shall we know before the night wind strays
Into town, leaving a sea-stale wake, and we close
Our eyes against desire's incoming tides?
Probably not. So let the unsayable have its way.
Let the moon rage and fade, as it will, and the heads
Of Queen Anne's lace bow down in the fields,
And the dark be praised. We shall be off,
Talking aloud to ourselves, repeating the words
That have always been used to describe our fate.

Itself Now

They will say it is feeling or mood, or the world, or the sound
The world makes on summer nights while everyone sleeps—
Trees awash with wind, something like that, something
As imprecise. But don't be fooled. The world
Is only a mirror returning its image. They will say
It is about particulars, making a case for this or that,
But it tries only to be itself. The low hills, the freshets,
The long dresses, even the lyre and dulcimer, mean nothing,
The music it makes is mainly its own. So far
From what it might be, it always turns into longing,
Spinning itself out for desire's sake, desire for its own end,
One word after another erasing the world and leaving instead
The invisible lines of its calling: Out there, out there.

Reading in Place

Imagine a poem that starts with a couple
Looking into a valley, seeing their house, the lawn
Out back with its wooden chairs, its shady patches of green,
Its wooden fence, and beyond the fence the rippled silver sheen
Of the local pond, its far side a tangle of sumac, crimson
In the fading light. Now imagine somebody reading the poem
And thinking, "I never guessed it would be like this,"
Then slipping it into the back of a book while the oblivious
Couple, feeling nothing is lost, not even the white
Streak of a flicker's tail that catches their eye, nor the slight
Toss of leaves in the wind, shift their gaze to the wooden dome
Of a nearby hill where the violet spread of dusk begins.
But the reader, out for a stroll in the autumn night, with all
The imprisoned sounds of nature dying around him, forgets
Not only the poem, but where he is, and thinks instead
Of a bleak Venetian mirror that hangs in a hall
By a curving stair, and how the stars in the sky's black glass
Sink down and the sea heaves them ashore like foam.
So much is adrift in the ever-opening rooms of elsewhere,
He cannot remember whose house it was, or when he was there.
Now imagine he sits years later under a lamp
And pulls a book from the shelf; the poem drops
To his lap. The couple are crossing a field
On their way home, still feeling that nothing is lost,
That they will continue to live harm-free, sealed
In the twilight's amber weather. But how will the reader know,
Especially now that he puts the poem, without looking,
Back in the book, the book where a poet stares at the sky
And says to a blank page, "Where, where in Heaven am I?"

The End

Not everyone knows what he shall sing at the end,
Watching the pier as the ship sails away, or what it will seem like
When he's held by the sea's roar, motionless, there at the end,
Or what he shall hope for once it is clear that he'll never go back.

When the time has passed to prune the rose or caress the cat,
When the sunset torching the lawn and the full moon icing it down
No longer appear, not everyone knows what he'll discover instead.
When the weight of the past leans against nothing, and the sky

Is no more than remembered light, and the stories of cirrus
And cumulus come to a close, and all the birds are suspended in flight,
Not everyone knows what is waiting for him, or what he shall sing
When the ship he is on slips into darkness, there at the end.

From *Dark Harbor*

I

In the night without end, in the soaking dark,
I am wearing a white suit that shines
Among the black leaves falling, among

The insect-covered moons of the streetlamps.
I am walking among the emerald trees
In the night without end. I am crossing

The street and disappearing around the corner.
I shine as I go through the park on my way
To the station where the others are waiting.

Soon we shall travel through the soundless dark,
With fires guiding us over the bitter terrain
Of the night without end. I am wearing

A suit that outdoes the moon, that is pure sheen
As I come to the station where the others
Are whispering, saying that the moon

Is no more a hindrance than anything else,
That, if anyone suffers, wings can be had
For a song or by trading arms, that the rules

On earth still hold for those about to depart,
That it is best to be ready, for the ash
Of the body is worthless and goes only so far.

VII

Oh you can make fun of the splendors of moonlight,
But what would the human heart be if it wanted
Only the dark, wanted nothing on earth

But the sea's ink or the rock's black shade?
On a summer night to launch yourself into the silver
Emptiness of air and look over the pale fields

At rest under the sullen stare of the moon,
And to linger in the depths of your vision and wonder
How in this whiteness what you love is past

Grief, and how in the long valley of your looking
Hope grows, and there, under the distant,
Barely perceptible fire of all the stars,

To feel yourself wake into change, as if your change
Were immense and figured into the heavens' longing.
And yet all you want is to rise out of the shade

Of yourself into the cooling blaze of a summer night
When the moon shines and the earth itself
Is covered and silent in the stoniness of its sleep.

VIII

If dawn breaks the heart, and the moon is a horror,
And the sun is nothing but the source of torpor,
Then of course I would have been silent all these years

And would not have chosen to go out tonight
In my new dark blue double-breasted suit
And to sit in a restaurant with a bowl

Of soup before me to celebrate how good life
Has been and how it has culminated in this instant.
The harmonies of wholesomeness have reached their apogee,

And I am aquiver with satisfaction, and you look
Good, too. I love your gold teeth and your dyed hair—
A little green, a little yellow—and your weight,

Which is finally up where we never thought
It would be. O my partner, my beautiful death,
My black paradise, my fusty intoxicant,

My symbolist muse, give me your breast
Or your hand or your tongue that sleeps all day
Behind its wall of reddish gums.

Lay yourself down on the restaurant floor
And recite all that's been kept from my happiness.
Tell me I have not lived in vain, that the stars

Will not die, that things will stay as they are,
That what I have seen will last, that I was not born
Into change, that what I have said has not been said for me.

XIV

The ship has been held in the harbor.
The promise of departure has begun to dim.
The radiance of the sea, the shining abundance

Of its blue, are nevertheless undiminished.
The will of the passengers struggles to release
The creaking ship. All they want

Is one last voyage beyond the papery palms
And the shoals of melancholy, beyond the glass
And alabaster mansions strung along

The shores, beyond the siren sounds
And the grinding gears of big trucks climbing the hills,
Out into the moonlit bareness of waves,

Where watery scrawls tempt the voyager to reach down
And hold the dissolving messages in his palm.
Again and again the writing surfaces,

Shines a moment in the light, then sinks unread.
Why should the passengers want so badly
To glimpse what they shall never have?

Why are so many of them crowded at the rail,
With the ship still dozing in the harbor?
And to whom are they waving? It has been

Years since the stores in town were open,
Years since the flag was raised in the little park,
Since the cloud behind the nearby mountain moved.

XVI

It is true, as someone has said, that in
A world without heaven all is farewell.
Whether you wave your hand or not,

It is farewell, and if no tears come to your eyes
It is still farewell, and if you pretend not to notice,
Hating what passes, it is still farewell.

Farewell no matter what. And the palms as they lean
Over the green, bright lagoon, and the pelicans
Diving, and the glistening bodies of bathers resting,

Are stages in an ultimate stillness, and the movement
Of sand, and of wind, and the secret moves of the body
Are part of the same, a simplicity that turns being

Into an occasion for mourning, or into an occasion
Worth celebrating, for what else does one do,
Feeling the weight of the pelicans' wings,

The density of the palms' shadows, the cells that darken
The backs of bathers? These are beyond the distortions
Of chance, beyond the evasions of music. The end

Is enacted again and again. And we feel it
In the temptations of sleep, in the moon's ripening,
In the wine as it waits in the glass.

XX

Is it you standing among the olive trees
Beyond the courtyard? You in the sunlight
Waving me closer with one hand while the other

Shields your eyes from the brightness that turns
All that is not you dead white? Is it you
Around whom the leaves scatter like foam?

You in the murmuring night that is scented
With mint and lit by the distant wilderness
Of stars? Is it you? Is it really you

Rising from the script of waves, the length
Of your body casting a sudden shadow over my hand
So that I feel how cold it is as it moves

Over the page? You leaning down and putting
Your mouth against mine so I should know
That a kiss is only the beginning

Of what until now we could only imagine?
Is it you or the long compassionate wind
That whispers in my ear: alas, alas?

XXII

It happened years ago and in somebody else's
Dining room. Madame X begged to be relieved
Of a sexual pain that had my name

Written all over it. Those were the days
When so many things of a sexual nature seemed to happen,
And my name—I believed—was written on all of them.

Madame X took my hand under the table, placed it
On her thigh, then moved it up. You would never know
What a woman with such blue eyes and blond hair

Was not wearing. Did I suffer,
Knowing that I was wanted for the wrong reasons?
Of course, and it has taken me years to recover

We don't give parties like that anymore.
These days we sit around and sigh.
We like the sound of it, and it seems to combine

Weariness and judgment, even to suggest
No eggs for the moment, no sausages either,
Just come, take me away, and put me to bed.

XXIII

And suddenly we heard the explosion.
A man who'd been cramped and bloated for weeks
Blew wide open. His wife, whose back was to him,

Didn't turn right away to give everything—
The cheese and soggy bread—a chance to settle.
She was a beauty, and considered a cunning cook,

But there were things she did not share with the rest of us.
So the fact that her back was turned was important.
We seemed to sense that she and her husband

Hadn't been seeing eye to eye. But that was as far as we got
Even though we questioned her culinary skills and what
Had driven her to blow up her husband, and we wondered—

Each of the men in the room—if she considered
Blowing us up. It happened that she left town
Before we could ask. No charges were pressed

So she sold the house and moved
To a large southern city where no one would know
The dangers of being invited to her house for dinner.

XXVII

Of this one I love how the beautiful echoed
Within the languorous length of his sentences,
Forming a pleasing pointless commotion;

Of another the figures pushing each other
Out of the way, the elaborate overcharged
Thought threatening always to fly apart;

Of another the high deliberate tone,
The diction tending toward falseness
But always falling perfectly short;

Of another the rush and vigor of observation,
The speed of disclosure, the aroused intelligence
Exerting itself, lifting the poem into prophecy;

Of this one the humor, the struggle to locate high art
Anywhere but where expected, and to gild the mundane
With the force of the demonic or the angelic;

Of yet another the precision, the pursuit of rightness,
Balance, some ineffable decorum, the measured, circuitous
Stalking of the subject, turning surprise to revelation;

And that leaves this one on the side of his mountain,
Hunched over the page, thanking his loves for coming
And keeping him company all this time.

XXVIII

There is a luminousness, a convergence of enchantments,
And the world is altered for the better as trees,
Rivers, mountains, animals, all find their true place,

But only while Orpheus sings. When the song is over
The world resumes its old flaws, and things are again
Mismatched and misplaced and the cruelty of men

Is tempered only by laws. Orpheus can change the world
For a while, but he cannot save it, which is his despair.
It is a brilliant limitation he enacts and

He knows it, which is why the current of his song
Is always mournful, always sad. It is even worse
For the rest of us. As someone has said, ". . . we barely begin

And paralysis takes over, forcing us out for a breath
Of fresh air." As if that wasn't bad enough, he says,
"But though reams of work do get done, not much listens.

I have the feeling my voice is just for me . . ." There is
A current of resignation that charges even our most
Determined productions. Still, we feel better for trying,

And there is always a glass of wine to restore us
To our former majesty, to the well of our wishes
In which we are mirrored, but darkly as though

A shadowed glass held within its frozen calm an image
Of abundance, a bloom of humanness, a hymn in which
The shapes and sounds of paradise are buried.

XXIX

The folded memory of our great and singular elevations,
The tragic slapping of vowels to produce tears,
The heavy golden grieving in our dreams,

Shaping the soul's solemn sounds on the edge of speech
That carry the fullness of intention and the emptiness
Of achievement, are not quite the savage

Knowledge of ourselves that refuses to correct itself
But lumbers instead into formless affirmation,
Saying selfhood is hating Dad or wanting Mom,

Is being kissed by a reader somewhere, is about me
And all my minutes circulating around me like flies—
Me at my foulest, the song of me, me in the haunted

Woods of my own condition, solitary but never alone.
These are bad times. Idiots have stolen the moonlight.
They cast their shadowy pomp wherever they wish.

XXXI

Here we are in Labrador. I've always
Wanted to be here, especially with you,
In this cabin, with a fire blazing. You are

Wearing a Calvin Klein suit and I am in
My father's velvet smoking jacket. That's all.
Why? Because I am happy. And I am ready

For the first sign from you that we should
Get into bed. These moments of giddy anticipation
Are the happiest of my life. I wonder if we

Are not part of someone's prediction of what
The world could be at its very best, if we,
In this frigid landscape free of shopping

Opportunities, are where the world is headed?
Or maybe we are part of the record of what
Has already happened, and are a sign of the depths

To which the world sank? Your costly suit,
My shabby jacket, this cabin without indoor
Plumbing or decent stove or stereo or TV

May be no more than a joke in the final
Tally of accomplishments to be claimed
At some late date. Still, here we are

And they can't take that away from us,
And if they laugh, so what, we're here,
Happy in Labrador, dancing into the wee hours.

XXXV

The sickness of angels is nothing new.
I have seen them crawling like bees,
Flightless, chewing their tongues, not singing,

Down by the bus terminal, hanging out,
Showing their legs, hiding their wings,
Carrying on for their brief term on earth,

No longer smiling; asleep in the shade of each other
They drift into the arms of strangers who step
Into their light, which is the mascara of Eden,

Offering more than invisible love,
Intangible comforts, offering the taste,
The pure erotic glory of death without echoes,

The feel of kisses blown out of heaven,
Melting the moment they land.

XXXVI

I cannot decide whether or not to stroll
Through the somber garden where the grass in the shade
Is silver and frozen and where the general green

Of the rest of the garden is dark except
For a luminous patch made by the light of a window.
I cannot decide, and because it is autumn

When the sadness of gardens is greatest, I believe
That someone is already there and is waiting
For the pale appearance of another. She sits

On one of the benches, breathing the sweet
Rotten odors of leaves trapped under the trees, and feels
The sudden cold, a seasonal chill, the distant breath

Of coming rain. So many silent battles are waged
By those who sit alone and wait, and by those who delay.
By the time I arrive the snow has whitened my hair,

And placed on my shoulders two glittering, tiny
Epaulettes. I could be a major in Napoleon's army,
Which might be the reason she asks me:

Why would someone invade a poor country
Like this, a garden near the end of its life
With a woman inside it, unless he was lonely

And would do what he must to stave off the long
Campaigns of unhappiness that level everything,
Making rebuilding impossible, especially in winter?

XXXIX

When after a long silence one picks up the pen
And leans over the paper and says to himself:
Today I shall consider Marsyas

Whose body was flayed to excess,
Who made no crime that would square
With what he was made to suffer.

Today I shall consider the shredded remains of Marsyas—
What do they mean as they gather the sunlight
That falls in pieces through the trees,

As in Titian's late painting? Poor Marsyas,
A body, a body of work as it turns and falls
Into suffering, becoming the flesh of light,

Which is fed to onlookers centuries later.
Can this be the cost of encompassing pain?
After a long silence, would I, whose body

Is whole, sheltered, kept in the dark by a mind
That prefers it that way, know what I'd done
And what its worth was? Or is a body scraped

From the bone of experience, the chart of suffering
To be read in such ways that all flesh might be redeemed,
At least for the moment, the moment it passes into song.

XL

How can I sing when I haven't the heart, or the hope
That something of paradise persists in my song,
That a touch of those long afternoons of summer

Flowing with golden greens under the sky's unbroken blue
Will find a home in yet another imagined place?
Will someone be there to play the viola, someone for whom

The sad tunes still matter? And after I go, as I must,
And come back through the hourglass, will I have proved
That I live against time, that the silk of the songs

I sang is not lost? Or will I have proved that whatever I love
Is unbearable, that the views of Lethe will never
Improve, that whatever I sing is a blank?

XLIII

All afternoon I have thought how alike
Are "The Lament of the Pianos Heard in Rich Neighborhoods"
And "Piano Practice at the Academy of the Holy Angels,"

And how the girls that played are no longer here. Yet it was never
A vast music that mingled with the lusters of the room,
Nothing that would drown our desire for rest or silence.

It was just there like the source of delight—
Unblemished, unobserved—though things did not always turn out
    well.
As now the green leaves brood under an early snow,

And the houses are darkened by time. The sounds of summer
Have left. The purple woods, which color the distance,
Form a farewell for the monotonous autumn.

The snows have come, and the black shapes of the pianos
Are sleeping and cannot be roused, like the girls themselves
Who have gone, and the leaves, and all that was just here.

XLIV

I recall that I stood before the breaking waves,
Afraid not of the water so much as the noise,
That I covered my ears and ran to my mother

And waited to be taken away to the house in town
Where it was quiet, with no sound of the sea anywhere near.
Yet the sea itself, the sight of it, the way it spread

As far as we could see, was thrilling.
Only its roar was frightening. And now years later
It is the sound as well as its size that I love

And miss in my inland exile among the mountains
That do not change except for the light
That colors them or the snows that make them remote

Or the clouds that lift them, so they appear much higher
Than they are. They are acted upon and have none
Of the mystery of the sea that generates its own changes.

Encounters with each are bound to differ,
Yet if I had to choose I would look at the sea
And lose myself in its sounds which so frightened me once.

But in those days what did I know of the pleasures of loss,
Of the edge of the abyss coming close with its hisses
And storms, a great watery animal breaking itself on the rocks,

Sending up stars of salt, loud clouds of spume.

XLV

I am sure you would find it misty here,
With lots of stone cottages badly needing repair.
Groups of souls, wrapped in cloaks, sit in the fields

Or stroll the winding unpaved roads. They are polite,
And oblivious to their bodies, which the wind passes through,
Making a shushing sound. Not long ago,

I stopped to rest in a place where an especially
Thick mist swirled up from the river. Someone,
Who claimed to have known me years before,

Approached, saying there were many poets
Wandering around who wished to be alive again.
They were ready to say the words they had been unable to say—

Words whose absence had been the silence of love,
Of pain, and even of pleasure. Then he joined a small group,
Gathered beside a fire. I believe I recognized

Some of the faces, but as I approached they tucked
Their heads under their wings. I looked away to the hills
Above the river, where the golden lights of sunset

And sunrise are one and the same, and saw something flying
Back and forth, fluttering its wings. Then it stopped in midair.
It was an angel, one of the good ones, about to sing.

From *Blizzard of One*

The Beach Hotel

Oh, look, the ship is sailing without us! And the wind
Is from the east, and the next ship leaves in a year.
Let's go back to the beach hotel where the rain never stops,
Where the garden, green and shadow-filled, says, in the rarest
Of whispers, "Beware of encroachment." We can stroll, can visit
The dead decked out in their ashen pajamas, and, after a tour
Of the birches, can lie on the rumpled bed, watching
The ancient moonlight creep across the floor. The windowpanes
Will shake, and waves of darkness, cold, uncalled-for, grim,
Will cover us. And into the close and mirrored catacombs of sleep
We'll fall, and there in the faded light discover the bones,
The dust, the bitter remains of someone who might have been
                    Had we not taken his place.

Old Man Leaves Party

It was clear when I left the party
That though I was over eighty I still had
A beautiful body. The moon shone down as it will
On moments of deep introspection. The wind held its breath.
And look, somebody left a mirror leaning against a tree.
Making sure that I was alone, I took off my shirt.
The flowers of bear grass nodded their moonwashed heads.
I took off my pants and the magpies circled the redwoods.
Down in the valley the creaking river was flowing once more.
How strange that I should stand in the wilds alone with my body.
I know what you are thinking. I was like you once. But now
With so much before me, so many emerald trees, and
Weed-whitened fields, mountains and lakes, how could I not
Be only myself, this dream of flesh, from moment to moment?

I Will Love the Twenty-first Century

Dinner was getting cold. The guests, hoping for quick,
Impersonal, random encounters of the usual sort, were sprawled
In the bedrooms. The potatoes were hard, the beans soft, the meat—
There was no meat. The winter sun had turned the elms and houses
   yellow;
Deer were moving down the road like refugees; and in the driveway,
   cats
Were warming themselves on the hood of a car. Then a man turned
And said to me: "Although I love the past, the dark of it,
The weight of it teaching us nothing, the loss of it, the all
Of it asking for nothing, I will love the twenty-first century more,
For in it I see someone in bathrobe and slippers, brown-eyed and poor,
Walking through snow without leaving so much as a footprint behind."
   "Oh," I said, putting my hat on. "Oh."

The Next Time

I

Nobody sees it happening, but the architecture of our time
Is becoming the architecture of the next time. And the dazzle

Of light upon the waters is as nothing beside the changes
Wrought therein, just as our waywardness means

Nothing against the steady pull of things over the edge.
Nobody can stop the flow, but nobody can start it either.

Time slips by; our sorrows do not turn into poems,
And what is invisible stays that way. Desire has fled,

Leaving only a trace of perfume in its wake,
And so many people we loved have gone,

And no voice comes from outer space, from the folds
Of dust and carpets of wind, to tell us that this

Is the way it was meant to happen, that if only we knew
How long the ruins would last we would never complain.

II

Perfection is out of the question for people like us,
So why plug away at the same old self when the landscape

Has opened its arms and given us marvelous shrines
To flock toward? The great motels to the west are waiting,

In somebody's yard a pristine dog is hoping that we'll drive by,
And on the rubber surface of a lake people bobbing up and down

Will wave. The highway comes right to the door, so let's
Take off before the world out there burns up. Life should be more

Than the body's weight working itself from room to room.
A turn through the forest will do us good, so will a spin

Among the farms. Just think of the chickens strutting,
The cows swinging their udders, and flicking their tails at flies.

And one can imagine prisms of summer light breaking against
The silent, haze-filled sleep of the farmer and his wife.

III

It could have been another story, the one that was meant
Instead of the one that happened. Living like this,

Hoping to revise what has been false or rendered unreadable,
Is not what we wanted. Believing that the intended story

Would have been like a day in the west when everything
Is tirelessly present—the mountains casting their long shadow

Over the valley where the wind sings its circular tune
And trees respond with a dry clapping of leaves—was overly

Simple no doubt, and short-sighted. For soon the leaves,
Having gone black, would fall, and the annulling snow

Would pillow the walk, and we, with shovels in hand, would meet,
Bow, and scrape the sidewalk clean. What else would there be

This late in the day for us but desire to make amends
And start again, the sun's compassion as it disappears?

The Night, the Porch

To stare at nothing is to learn by heart
What all of us will be swept into, and baring oneself
To the wind is feeling the ungraspable somewhere close by.
Trees can sway or be still. Day or night can be what they wish.
What we desire, more than a season or weather, is the comfort
Of being strangers, at least to ourselves. This is the crux
Of the matter, which is why even now we seem to be waiting
For something whose appearance would be its vanishing—
The sound, say, of a few leaves falling, or just one leaf,
Or less. There is no end to what we can learn. The book out there
Tells us as much, and was never written with us in mind.

Our Masterpiece Is the Private Life

I

Is there something down by the water keeping itself from us,
Some shy event, some secret of the light that falls upon the deep,
Some source of sorrow that does not wish to be discovered yet?

Why should we care? Doesn't desire cast its rainbows over the coarse
    porcelain
Of the world's skin and with its measures fill the air? Why look for
    more?

II

And now, while the advocates of awfulness and sorrow
Push their dripping barge up and down the beach, let's eat
Our brill, and sip this beautiful white Beaune.

True, the light is artificial, and we are not well-dressed.
So what. We like it here. We like the bullocks in the field next door,
We like the sound of wind passing over grass. The way you speak,

In that low voice, our late-night disclosures . . . why live
For anything else? Our masterpiece is the private life.]

III

Standing on the quay between the *Roving Swan* and the *Star
    Immaculate,*

Breathing the night air as the moment of pleasure taken
In pleasure vanishing seems to grow, its self-soiling

Beauty, which can only be what it was, sustaining itself
A little longer in its going, I think of our own smooth passage
Through the graded partitions, the crises that bleed

Into the ordinary, leaving us a little more tired each time,
A little more distant from the experiences, which, in the old days,
Held us captive for hours. The drive along the winding road

Back to the house, the sea pounding against the cliffs,
The glass of whiskey on the table, the open book, the questions,
All the day's rewards waiting at the doors of sleep . . .

Morning, Noon, and Night

I

And the morning green, and the buildup of weather, and my brows
Have not been brushed, and never will be, by the breezes of divinity.
That much is clear, at least to me, but yesterday I noticed
Something floating in and out of clouds, something like a bird,
But also like a man, black-suited, with his arms outspread.
And I thought this could be a sign that I've been wrong. Then I woke,
And on my bed the shadow of the future fell, and on the liquid ruins
Of the sea outside, and on the shells of buildings at the water's edge.
A rapid overcast blew in, bending trees and flattening fields. I stayed
     in bed,
Hoping it would pass. What might have been still waited for its
     chance.

II

Whatever the star charts told us to watch for or the maps
Said we would find, nothing prepared us for what we discovered.
We toiled away in the shadowless depths of noon,
While an alien wind slept in the branches, and dead leaves
Turned to dust in the streets. Cities of light, long summers
Of leisure, were not to be ours; for to come as we had, long after
It mattered, to live among tombs, great as they are,
Was to be no nearer the end, no farther from where we began.

III

These nights of pinks and purples vanishing, of freakish heat
That strokes our skin until we fall asleep and stray to places
We hoped would always be beyond our reach—the deeps
Where nothing flourishes, where everything that happens seems
To be for keeps. We sweat, and plead to be released
Into the coming day on time, and panic at the thought
Of never getting there and being forced to drift forgotten
On a midnight sea where every thousand years a ship is sighted, or
    a swan,
Or a drowned swimmer whose imagination has outlived his fate, and
    who swims
To prove, to no one in particular, how false his life had been.

A Piece of the Storm

for Sharon Horvath

From the shadow of domes in the city of domes,
A snowflake, a blizzard of one, weightless, entered your room
And made its way to the arm of the chair where you, looking up
From your book, saw it the moment it landed. That's all
There was to it. No more than a solemn waking
To brevity, to the lifting and falling away of attention, swiftly,
A time between times, a flowerless funeral. No more than that
Except for the feeling that this piece of the storm,
Which turned into nothing before your eyes, would come back,
That someone years hence, sitting as you are now, might say:
It's time. The air is ready. The sky has an opening.

A Suite of Appearances

for Octavio and Marie Jo Paz

I

Out of what dark or lack has he come to wait
At the edge of your gaze for the moment when you
Would look up and see through the trembling leaves

His shadow suddenly there? Out of what place has he come
To enter the light that remains, and say in the weightless
Cadence of those who arrive from a distance that the crossing

Was hard with only a gleam to follow over the Sea of Something,
Which opens and closes, breaks and flashes, spreading its cold,
Watery foliage wherever it can to catch you and carry you

And leave you where you have never been, that he has escaped
To tell you with all that is left of his voice that this is his
Story, which continues wherever the end is happening?

II

No wonder—since things come into view then drop from sight—
We clear a space for ourselves, a stillness where nothing
Is blurred: a common palm, and oasis in which to rest, to sit

For hours beside the pool while the moonlight builds its palaces,
And columns rise, and coral chambers open onto patios
With songbirds practicing their peeps and trills.

225

No wonder the evening paper lies unread, no wonder what happened
Before tonight, the history of ourselves, leaves us cold.

III

How it comes forward, and deposits itself like wind
In the ear which hears only the humming at first, the first
Suggestion of what is to come, how it grows out of itself,

Out of the humming because if it didn't it would die
In the graveyard of sound without being known, and then
Nothing would happen for days or weeks until something like it

Came back, a sound announcing itself as your own, a voice
That is yours, bending under the weight of desire,
Suddenly turning your language into a field unfolding

And all the while the humming can still be detected, the original
Humming before it was yours, and you lie back and hear it,
Surprised that what you are saying was something you meant,

And you think that perhaps you are not who you thought, that
    henceforth
Any idea of yourself must include a body surrounding a song.

IV

In another time, we will want to know how the earth looked
Then, and were people the way we are now. In another time,
The records they left will convince us that we are unchanged

And could be at ease in the past, and not alone in the present.
And we shall be pleased. But beyond all that, what cannot
Be seen or explained will always be elsewhere, always supposed,

Invisible even beneath the signs—the beautiful surface,
The uncommon knowledge—that point its way. In another time,
What cannot be seen will define us, and we shall be prompted

To say that language is error, and all things are wronged
By representation. The self, we shall say, can never be
Seen with a disguise, and never be seen without one.

v

To sit in this chair and wonder where is endlessness
Born, where does it go, how close has it come; and to see
The snow coming down, the flakes enlarging whatever they touch,

Changing shapes until no shape remains. In their descent
They are like stars overtaken by light, or like thoughts
That drift before the long, blank windows facing the future,

Withering, whirling, continuing down, finally away
From the clear panes into the place where nothing will do,
Where nothing is needed or said because it is already known.

And when it is over, and the deep, unspeakable reaches of white
Melt into memory, how will the warmth of the fire,
So long in coming, keep us from mourning the loss?

VI

Of occasions flounced with rose and gold in which the sun
Sinks deep and drowns in a blackening sea, of those, and more,
To be tired. To have the whole sunset again, moment by moment,

As it occurred, in a correct and detailed account, only darkens
Our sense of what happened. There is a limit to what we can picture
And to how much of a good thing is a good thing. Better to hope

For the merest reminder, a spectral glimpse—there but not there,
Something not quite a scene, poised only to be dissolved,
So, when it goes as it must, no sense of loss springs in its wake.

The houses, the gardens, the roaming dogs, let them become
The factors of absence, an incantation of the ineffable.
The backyard was red, that much we know. And the church bell

Tolled the hour. What more is there? The odors of food,
The last traces of dinner, are gone. The glasses are washed.
The neighborhood sleeps. Will the same day ever come back, and
    with it

Our amazement at having been in it, or will only a dark haze
Spread at the back of the mind, erasing events, one after
The other, so brief they may have been lost to begin with?

Here

The sun that silvers all the buildings here
Has slid behind a cloud, and left the once bright air
Something less than blue. Yet everything is clear.
Across the road, some dead plants dangle down from rooms
Unoccupied for months, two empty streets converge
On a central square, and on a nearby hill some tombs,
Half buried in a drift of wild grass, appear to merge
With houses at the edge of town. A breeze
Stirs up some dust, turns up a page or two, then dies.
All the boulevards are lined with leafless trees.
There are no dogs nosing around, no birds, no buzzing flies.
Dust gathers everywhere—on stools and bottles in the bars,
On shelves and racks of clothing in department stores,
On the blistered dashboards of abandoned cars.
Within the church, whose massive, rotting doors
Stay open, it is cool, so if a visitor should wander in
He could easily relax, kneel and pray,
Or watch the dirty light pour through the baldachin,
Or think about the heat outside that does not go away,
Which might be why there are no people there—who knows—
Or about the dragon that he saw when he arrived,
Curled up before its cave in saurian repose,
And about how good it is to be survived.

Two de Chiricos

for Harry Ford

I   THE PHILOSOPHER'S CONQUEST

This melancholy moment will remain,
So, too, the oracle beyond the gate,
And always the tower, the boat, the distant train.

Somewhere to the south a duke is slain,
A war is won. Here, it is too late.
This melancholy moment will remain.

Here, an autumn evening without rain,
Two artichokes abandoned on a crate,
And always the tower, the boat, the distant train.

Is this another scene of childhood pain?
Why do the clockhands say 1:28?
This melancholy moment will remain.

The green and yellow light of love's domain
Falls upon the joylessness of fate,
And always the tower, the boat, the distant train.

The things our vision wills us to contain,
The life of objects, their unbearable weight.
This melancholy moment will remain,
And always the tower, the boat, the distant train.

Boredom sets in first, and then despair.
One tries to brush it off. It only grows.
Something about the silence of the square.

Something is wrong; something about the air,
Its color; about the light, the way it glows.
Boredom sets in first, and then despair.

The muses in their fluted evening wear,
Their faces blank, might lead one to suppose
Something about the silence of the square,

Something about the buildings standing there.
But no, they have no purpose but to pose.
Boredom sets in first, and then despair.

What happens after that, one doesn't care.
What brought one here— the desire to compose
Something about the silence of the square,

Or something else, of which one's not aware,
Life itself, perhaps—who really knows?
Boredom sets in first, and then despair . . .
Something about the silence of the square.

Some Last Words

1

It is easier for a needle to pass through a camel
Than for a poor man to enter a woman of means.
Just go to the graveyard and ask around.

2

Eventually, you slip outside, letting the door
Bang shut on your latest thought. What was it anyway?
Just go to the graveyard and ask around.

3

"Negligence" is the perfume I love.
O Fedora. Fedora. If you want any,
Just go to the graveyard and ask around.

4

The bones of the buffalo, the rabbit at sunset,
The wind and its double, the tree, the town . . .
Just go to the graveyard and ask around.

5

If you think good things are on their way
And the world will improve, don't hold your breath.
Just go to the graveyard and ask around.

6

You over there, why do you ask if this is the valley
Of limitless blue, and if we are its prisoners?
Just go to the graveyard and ask around.

7

Life is a dream that is never recalled when the sleeper awakes.
If this is beyond you, Magnificent One,
Just go to the graveyard and ask around.

In Memory of Joseph Brodsky

It could be said, even here, that what remains of the self
Unwinds into a vanishing light, and thins like dust, and heads
To a place where knowing and nothing pass into each other, and
    through;
That it moves, unwinding still, beyond the vault of brightness ended,
And continues to a place which may never be found, where the
    unsayable,
Finally, once more is uttered, but lightly, quickly, like random rain
That passes in sleep, that one imagines passes in sleep.
What remains of the self unwinds and unwinds, for none
Of the boundaries holds—neither the shapeless one between us,
Nor the one that falls between your body and your voice. Joseph,
Dear Joseph, those sudden reminders of your having been—the
    places
And times whose greatest life was the one you gave them—now
    appear
Like ghosts in your wake. What remains of the self unwinds
Beyond us, for whom time is only a measure of meanwhile
And the future no more than et cetera et cetera . . . but fast and
    forever.

What It Was

It was impossible to imagine, impossible
Not to imagine; the blueness of it, the shadow it cast,
Falling downward, filling the dark with the chill of itself,
The cold of it falling out of itself, out of whatever idea
Of itself it described as it fell; a something, a smallness,
A dot, a speck, a speck within a speck, an endless depth
Of smallness; a song, but less than a song, something drowning
Into itself, something going, a flood of sound, but less
Than a sound; the last of it, the blank of it,
The tender small blank of it filling its echo, and falling,
And rising unnoticed, and falling again, and always thus,
And always because, and only because, once having been, it was . . .

II

It was the beginning of a chair;
It was the gray couch; it was the walls,
The garden, the gravel road; it was the way
The ruined moonlight fell across her hair.
It was that, and it was more. It was the wind that tore
At the trees; it was the fuss and clutter of clouds, the shore
Littered with stars. It was the hour which seemed to say
That if you knew what time it really was, you would not
Ask for anything again. It was that. It was certainly that.
It was also what never happened—a moment so full
That when it went, as it had to, no grief was large enough

To contain it. It was the room that appeared unchanged
After so many years. It was that. It was the hat
She'd forgotten to take, the pen she left on the table.
It was the sun on my hand. It was the sun's heat. It was the way
I sat, the way I waited for hours, for days. It was that. Just that.

The Delirium Waltz

I cannot remember when it began. The lights were low. We were walking across the floor, over polished wood and inlaid marble, through shallow water, through dustings of snow, through cloudy figures of fallen light. I cannot remember but I think you were there—whoever you were—sometimes with me, sometimes watching. Shapes assembled themselves and dissolved. The hall to the ballroom seemed endless, and a voice—perhaps it was yours—was saying we'd never arrive. Now we were gliding over the floor, our clothes were heavy, the music was slow, and I thought we would die all over again. I believe we were happy. We moved in the drift of sound, and whether we went toward the future or back to the past we weren't able to tell. Anxiety has its inflections—wasteful, sad, tragic at times—but here it had none. In its harmless hovering it was merely fantastic, so we kept dancing. I think I was leading. Why else would I practice those near calamitous dips? I think it was clear that we had always been dancing, always been eager to give ourselves to the rapture of music. Even the simplest movement, from the wafting of clouds to the wink of an eye, could catch and hold our attention. The rooms became larger and finally dimensionless, and we kept gliding, gliding and turning.

> And then came Bob and Sonia
> And the dance was slow
> And joining them now were Chip and Molly
> And Joseph dear Joseph was dancing and smoking
>
> And the dance was slow
> And into the hall years later came Tom and Em

And Joseph dear Joseph was dancing and smoking
And Bill and Sandy were leaning together

And into the hall years later came Tom and Em
Holding each other and turning and turning
And Bill and Sandy were leaning together
And Wally and Deb and Jorie and Jim

Holding each other and turning and turning
Then came Jules tall and thin
And Wally and Deb and Jorie and Jim
Everyone moving everyone dancing

Then came Jules tall and thin
Across the wide floor
Everyone moving everyone dancing
Harry was there and so was Kathleen

Across the wide floor
Looking better than ever came Jessie and Steve
Harry was there and so was Kathleen
And Peter and Barbara had just gotten back

Looking better than ever came Jessie and Steve
Leon and Judith Muffie and Jim
And Peter and Barbara had just gotten back
And others were there

Leon and Judith Muffie and Jim
Charlie and Helen were eating and dancing
And others were there
Wearing their best

Charlie and Helen were eating and dancing
Glenn and Angela Buck and Cathy
Wearing their best
Around and around dancing and dancing

And our shadows floated away toward sunset and darkened the backs
of birds, and blackened the sea whose breath smelled slightly of fish, of
almonds, of rotting fruit. Soon the air was soiled with dust and purple
clouds. We were standing, watching everyone else afloat on the floor,
on the sea of the floor, like a raft of voices. "Hello," they said, as they
sailed by, "may we have this dance?" And off they went to another
room with pale blue walls and birds.

And one room led to another
And birds flew back and forth
People roamed the veranda
Under the limbs of trees

And birds flew back and forth
A golden haze was everywhere
Under the limbs of trees
And Howie was there with Francine

A golden haze was everywhere
And Jeannette and Buddy were dancing
And Howie was there with Francine
Angels must always be pale they said

And Jeannette and Buddy were dancing
And Louise and Karen were talking
Angels must always be pale they said
But pale turns round to white

And Louise and Karen were talking
Saying that blue slides into black
But pale turns round to white
And Jules was there in heels

Saying that blue slides into black
Rosanna was there and Maria
And Jules was there in heels
And day and night were one

Rosanna was there and Maria
And Rusty and Carol were there
And day and night were one
And the sea's green body was near

And Rusty and Carol were there
And Charles and Holly were dancing
And the sea's green body was near
Hello out there hello

And Charles and Holly were dancing
So thin they were and light
Hello out there hello
Can anyone hear out there

And the rush of water was loud as if the ballroom were flooded. And I was dancing alone in the absence of all that I knew and was bound by. And here was the sea—the blur, the erasure of difference, the end of self, the end of whatever surrounds the self. And I kept going. The breakers flashed and fell under the moon's gaze. Scattered petals of foam shone briefly, then sank in the sand. It was cold, and I found myself suddenly back with the others. That vast ungraspable body, the sea, that huge and meaningless empire of water, was left on its own.

They drifted over the floor
And the silver sparkled a little
Oh how they moved together
The crystals shook in the draft

And the silver sparkled a little
So many doors were open
The crystals shook in the draft
Nobody knew what would happen

So many doors were open
And there was Eleanor dancing
Nobody knew what would happen
Now Red waltzed into the room

And there was Eleanor dancing
And Don and Jean were waiting
Now Red waltzed into the room
The years would come and go

And Don and Jean were waiting
Hours and hours would pass
The years would come and go
The palms in the hallway rustled

Hours and hours would pass
Now enter the children of Em
The palms in the hallway rustled
And here were the children of Tom

Now enter the children of Em
There was nothing to do but dance
And here were the children of Tom
And Nolan was telling them something

There was nothing to do but dance
They would never sit down together
And Nolan was telling them something
And many who wished they could

Would never sit down together
The season of dancing was endless
And many who wished they could
Would never be able to stop

I cannot remember when it began. The lights were low. We were walking across the floor, over polished wood and inlaid marble, through shallow water, through dustings of snow, through cloudy figures of fallen light. I cannot remember, but I think you were there, whoever you were.

The View

for Derek Walcott

This is the place. The chairs are white. The table shines.
The person sitting there stares at the waxen glow.
The wind moves the air around, repeatedly,
As if to clear a space. "A space for me," he thinks.
He's always been drawn to the weather of leave-taking,
Arranging itself so that grief—even the most intimate—
Might be read from a distance. A long shelf of cloud
Hangs above the open sea with the sun, the sun
Of no distinction, sinking behind it—a mild version
Of the story that is told just once if true, and always too late.
The waitress brings his drink, which he holds
Against the waning light, but just for a moment.
Its red reflection tints his shirt. Slowly the sky becomes darker,
The wind relents, the view sublimes. The violet sweep of it
Seems, in this effortless nightfall, more than a reason
For being there, for seeing it, seems itself a kind
Of happiness, as if that plain fact were enough and would last.

From *Man and Camel*

The King

I went to the middle of the room and called out,
"I know you're here," then noticed him in the corner,
looking tiny in his jeweled crown and his cape
with ermine trim. "I have lost my desire to rule,"
he said. "My kingdom is empty except for you,
and all you do is ask for me." "But Your Majesty—"
"Don't 'Your Majesty' me," he said, and tilted his head
to one side and closed his eyes. "There," he whispered,
"that's more like it," and he entered his dream
like a mouse vanishing into its hole.

I Had Been a Polar Explorer

I had been a polar explorer in my youth
and spent countless days and nights freezing
in one blank place and then another. Eventually,
I quit my travels and stayed at home,
and there grew within me a sudden excess of desire,
as if a brilliant stream of light of the sort one sees
within a diamond were passing through me.
I filled page after page with visions of what I had witnessed—
groaning seas of pack ice, giant glaciers, and the windswept white
of icebergs. Then, with nothing more to say, I stopped
and turned my sights on what was near. Almost at once,
a man wearing a dark coat and broad-brimmed hat
appeared under the trees in front of my house.
The way he stared straight ahead and stood,
not shifting his weight, letting his arms hang down
at his side, made me think that I knew him.
But when I raised my hand to say hello,
he took a step back, turned away, and started to fade
as longing fades until nothing is left of it.

Man and Camel

On the eve of my fortieth birthday
I sat on the porch having a smoke
when out of the blue a man and a camel
happened by. Neither uttered a sound
at first, but as they drifted up the street
and out of town the two of them began to sing.
Yet what they sang is still a mystery to me—
the words were indistinct and the tune
too ornamental to recall. Into the desert
they went and as they went their voices
rose as one above the sifting sound
of windblown sand. The wonder of their singing,
its elusive blend of man and camel, seemed
an ideal image for all uncommon couples.
Was this the night that I had waited for
so long? I wanted to believe it was,
but just as they were vanishing, the man
and camel ceased to sing, and galloped
back to town. They stood before my porch,
staring up at me with beady eyes, and said:
"You ruined it. You ruined it forever."

Fire

Sometimes there would be a fire and I would walk into it
and come out unharmed and continue on my way,
and for me it was just another thing to have done.
As for putting out the fire, I left that to others
who would rush into the billowing smoke with brooms
and blankets to smother the flames. When they were through
they would huddle together to talk of what they had seen—
how lucky they were to have witnessed the lusters of heat,
the hushing effect of ashes, but even more to have known the
     fragrance
of burning paper, the sound of words breathing their last.

The Rose

The sorrows of the rose were mounting up.
Twisted in a field of weeds, the helpless rose
felt the breeze of paradise just once, then died.
The children cried, "Oh rose, come back.
We love you, rose." Then someone said that soon
they'd have another rose. "Come, my darlings,
down to the pond, lean over the edge, and look
at yourselves looking up. Now do you see it,
its petals open, rising to the surface, turning into you?"
"Oh no," they said. "We are what we are—nothing else."

How perfect. How ancient. How past repair.

Storm

On the last night of our house arrest
a howling wind tore through the streets,
ripping down shutters, scattering roof tiles,
leaving behind a river of refuse. When the sun
rose over the marble gate, I could see the guards,
sluggish in the morning heat, desert their posts
and stagger toward the woods just out of town.
"Darling," I said, "let's go, the guards have left,
the place is a ruin." But she was oblivious.
"You go," she said, and she pulled up the sheet
to cover her eyes. I ran downstairs and called
for my horse. "To the sea," I whispered, and off
we went and how quick we were, my horse and I,
riding over the fresh green fields, as if to our freedom.

Afterwords

Packs of wild dogs roamed the streets of the very rich,
looking for scraps that might have been thrown their way
by a caring cook or merciful maid. Birds flew in
from everywhere, going up and down and side to side.
In the distance, beyond the stucco mansions
with their patios and pools, beyond the cemetery
with its marble angels, barely visible to the naked eye,
a man was scaling a cliff, then stopped and turned, and
opened his mouth to scream, but when the screams arrived
they were faint and cold, no different from the snow
that kept on falling through the windless night.

They rushed from their houses to welcome the spring,
then ran to the piers to gaze at the backs of fish,
long and glistening, then to the stables to see
the sleek, cloud-breathing horses. Nothing could keep them
from their joy, neither the storm gathering strength
in the west nor the bombs going off in the east;
theirs was the bliss of another age. Suddenly,
a woman appeared on the beach and said that soon
she would sing. "Soon she will sing," murmured
the gathering crowd. "Soon she will sing," I said
to myself as I woke. Then I went to the window
and a river of old people with canes and flashlights
were inching their way down through the dark to the sea.

3

Twenty crows sat on the limbs of an elm.
The air was so clear that one could see up
the broad valley of patchwork fields to the next town
where a train releasing a ribbon of steam
pulled out of a small wood station. Minutes later,
a man stepped onto the platform, waited, then lifted
his suitcase over his head and hurled it onto the tracks.
"That's that," he said, and turned and walked away.
The crows had taken off, it was cold, and up ahead
long, windblown shadows lashed the passive ground.

Elevator

1

The elevator went to the basement. The doors opened.
A man stepped in and asked if I was going up.
"I'm going down," I said. "I won't be going up."

2

The elevator went to the basement. The doors opened.
A man stepped in and asked if I was going up.
"I'm going down," I said. "I won't be going up."

Black Sea

One clear night while the others slept, I climbed
the stairs to the roof of the house and under a sky
strewn with stars I gazed at the sea, at the spread of it,
the rolling crests of it raked by the wind, becoming
like bits of lace tossed in the air. I stood in the long,
whispering night, waiting for something, a sign, the approach
of a distant light, and I imagined you coming closer,
the dark waves of your hair mingling with the sea,
and the dark became desire, and desire the arriving light.
The nearness, the momentary warmth of you as I stood
on that lonely height watching the slow swells of the sea
break on the shore and turn briefly into glass and disappear . . .
Why did I believe you would come out of nowhere? Why with all
that the world offers would you come only because I was here?

Mother and Son

The son enters the mother's room
and stands by the bed where the mother lies.
The son believes that she wants to tell him
what he longs to hear—that he is her boy,
always her boy. The son leans down to kiss
the mother's lips, but her lips are cold.
The burial of feelings has begun. The son
touches the mother's hands one last time,
then turns and sees the moon's full face.
An ashen light falls across the floor.
If the moon could speak, what would it say?
If the moon could speak, it would say nothing.

Mirror

A white room and a party going on
and I was standing with some friends
under a large gilt-framed mirror
that tilted slightly forward
over the fireplace.
We were drinking whiskey
and some of us, feeling no pain,
were trying to decide
what precise shade of yellow
the setting sun turned our drinks.
I closed my eyes briefly,
then looked up into the mirror:
a woman in a green dress leaned
against the far wall.
She seemed distracted,
the fingers of one hand
fidgeted with her necklace,
and she was staring into the mirror,
not at me, but past me, into a space
that might be filled by someone
yet to arrive, who at that moment
could be starting the journey
which would lead eventually to her.
Then, suddenly, my friends
said it was time to move on.
This was years ago,
and though I have forgotten
where we went and who we all were,

I still recall that moment of looking up
and seeing the woman stare past me
into a place I could only imagine,
and each time it is with a pang,
as if just then I were stepping
from the depths of the mirror
into that white room, breathless and eager,
only to discover too late
that she is not there.

Moon

Open the book of evening to the page
where the moon, always the moon, appears

between two clouds, moving so slowly that hours
will seem to have passed before you reach the next page

where the moon, now brighter, lowers a path
to lead you away from what you have known

into those places where what you had wished for happens,
its lone syllable like a sentence poised

at the edge of sense, waiting for you to say its name
once more as you lift your eyes from the page

and close the book, still feeling what it was like
to dwell in that light, that sudden paradise of sound.

Marsyas

Something was wrong
Screams could be heard
In the morning dark
It was cold

Screams could be heard
A storm was coming
It was cold
And the screams were piercing

A storm was coming
Someone was struggling
And the screams were piercing
Hard to imagine

Someone was struggling
So close, so close
Hard to imagine
A man was tearing open his body

So close, so close
The screams were unbearable
A man was tearing open his body
What could we do

The screams were unbearable
His flesh was in ribbons
What could we do
The rain came down

His flesh was in ribbons
And nobody spoke
The rain came down
There were flashes of lightning

And nobody spoke
Trees shook in the wind
There were flashes of lightning
Then came thunder

My Name

Once when the lawn was a golden green
and the marbled moonlit trees rose like fresh memorials
in the scented air, and the whole countryside pulsed
with the chirr and murmur of insects, I lay in the grass,
feeling the great distances open above me, and wondered
what I would become and where I would find myself,
and though I barely existed, I felt for an instant
that the vast star-clustered sky was mine, and I heard
my name as if for the first time, heard it the way
one hears the wind or the rain, but faint and far off
as though it belonged not to me but to the silence
from which it had come and to which it would go.

Poem After the Seven Last Words

1

The story of the end, of the last word
of the end, when told, is a story that never ends.
We tell it and retell it—one word, then another
until it seems that no last word is possible,
that none would be bearable. Thus, when the hero
of the story says to himself, as to someone far away,
"Forgive them, for they know not what they do,"
we may feel that he is pleading for us, that we are
the secret life of the story and, as long as his plea
is not answered, we shall be spared. So the story
continues. So we continue. And the end, once more,
becomes the next, and the next after that.

2

There is an island in the dark, a dreamt-of place
where the muttering wind shifts over the white lawns
and riffles the leaves of trees, the high trees
that are streaked with gold and line the walkways there;
and those already arrived are happy to be the silken
remains of something they were but cannot recall;
they move to the sound of stars, which is also imagined,
but who cares about that; the polished columns they see
may be no more than shafts of sunlight, but for those
who live on and on in the radiance of their remains
this is of little importance. There is an island

in the dark and you will be there, I promise you, you
shall be with me in paradise, in the single season of being,
in the place of forever, you shall find yourself. And there
the leaves will turn and never fall, there the wind
will sing and be your voice as if for the first time.

3

Someday someone will write a story telling
among other things of a parting between mother
and son, of how she wandered off, of how he vanished
in air. But before that happens, it will describe
how their faces shone with a feeble light and how
the son was moved to say, "Woman, look at your son,"
then to a friend nearby, "Son, look at your mother."
At which point the writer will put down his pen
and imagine that while those words were spoken
something else happened, something unusual like
a purpose revealed, a secret exchanged, a truth
to which they, the mother and son, would be bound,
but what it was no one would know. Not even the writer.

4

These are the days of spring when the sky is filled
with the odor of lilac, when darkness becomes desire,
and there is nothing that does not wish to be born;
days when the fate of the present is a breezy fullness,
when the world's great gift for fiction gilds even
the dirt we walk on, and we feel we could live forever
while knowing of course that we can't. Such is our plight.
The master of weather and everything else, if he wants,
can bring forth a dark of a different kind, one hidden

by darkness so deep it cannot be seen. No one escapes.
Not even the man who believed he was chosen to do so,
for when the dark came down he cried out, "Father, Father,
why have you forsaken me?" To which no answer came.

5

To be thirsty. To say, "I thirst."
To close one's eyes and see the giant world
that is born each time the eyes are closed.
To see one's death. To see the darkening clouds
as the tragic cloth of a day of mourning. To be the one
mourned. To open the dictionary of the Beyond and discover
what one suspected, that the only word in it
is nothing. To try to open one's eyes, but not to be
able to. To feel the mouth burn. To feel the sudden
presence of what, again and again, was not said.
To translate it and have it remain unsaid. To know
at last that nothing is more real than nothing.

6

"It is finished," he said. You could hear him say it,
the words almost a whisper, then not even that,
but an echo so faint it seemed no longer to come
from him, but from elsewhere. This was his moment,
his final moment. "It is finished," he said into a vastness
that led to an even greater vastness, and yet all of it
within him. He contained it all. That was the miracle,
to be both large and small in the same instant, to be
like us, but more so, then finally to give up the ghost,
which is what happened. And from the storm that swirled
in his wake a formal nakedness took shape, the truth
of disguise and the mask of belief were joined forever.

7

Back down these stairs to the same scene,
to the moon, the stars, the night wind. Hours pass
and only the harp off in the distance and the wind
moving through it. And soon the sun's gray disk,
darkened by clouds, sailing above. And beyond,
as always, the sea of endless transparence, of utmost
calm, a place of constant beginning that has within it
what no eye has seen, what no ear has heard, what no hand
has touched, what has not arisen in the human heart.
To that place, to the keeper of that place, I commit myself.

A Note About the Author

Mark Strand was born in Summerside, Prince Edward Island, and was raised and educated in the United States. He is the author of eleven earlier books of poems, a book of stories, three volumes of translations, and monographs on the artists William Bailey and Edward Hopper. He has also edited a number of anthologies, most recently *100 Great Poems of the Twentieth Century*. He has received many honors and awards for his poetry, including a MacArthur Fellowship, the Pulitzer Prize (for *Blizzard of One*), and the Bollingen Prize. In 1990 he was chosen Poet Laureate of the United States. A longtime resident of Chicago, he now lives in New York City and teaches at Columbia University.

A Note on the Type

This book was set in Janson, a typeface long thought to have been made by the Dutchman Anton Janson, who was a practicing typefounder in Leipzig during the years 1668–1687. However, it has been conclusively demonstrated that these types are actually the work of Nicholas Kis (1650–1702), a Hungarian, who most probably learned his trade from the master Dutch typefounder Dirk Voskens. The type is an excellent example of the influential and sturdy Dutch types that prevailed in England up to the time William Caslon (1692–1766) developed his own incomparable designs from them.

Composed by Stratford Publishing Services,
Brattleboro, Vermont
Printed and bound by Thomson-Shore, Inc.,
Dexter, Michigan
Designed by Anthea Lingeman